WHEN THE
NEW DEAL
WAS YOUNG AND GAY

WHEN THE
NEW DEAL
WAS YOUNG AND GAY

Charles Hurd

Foreword by

JAMES A. FARLEY

HAWTHORN BOOKS, INC. *Publishers* New York and London

First Edition, September, 1965

Cartoons: Wide World, UPI

Frontispiece: David Stone Martin

H-9396

Foreword

DURING MY MORE THAN FIFTY YEARS in American politics I have noticed certain patterns. It seems to me that American politics is much like the sea which consantly rebalances itself: hurricanes raise mighty waves, but the sea is so delicate that even the tiniest breeze will cause a ripple. Great political leaders are much like skilled ship captains. They have as much respect for the will of the people as a good captain has for the sea. A good politician—like a good captain—knows that the very force which sustains him can also sink him.

Franklin D. Roosevelt was elected to the Presidency of the United States during one of this country's worst hurricanes; the economic organization of our country had broken down. He proved an excellent seaman.

In a very real sense, the country had to call on its greatest asset—the faith of the American people in their government. With the economic world crashing about us, everyone knew that the means of solution could only be in one thing: the honor of the U. S. Government and the marshaling of its strength by its President.

At that time, the office of the President of the United States assumed new proportions. This wide expansion was not a reaching for power. It was born of national necessity, not out of soaring personal ambitions. That necessity has not contracted. On the contrary, it has grown greater and greater. President Andrew Jackson first pointed out that the President and the Vice-President are the only offices filled by the election of the American people as a whole. Thus, the President is the sole spokesman for the entire nation.

Contrary to a widely held opinion, the great leaders of both parties place the nation over and above any party considerations. The fact that I was not a particular admirer of the policies of the Republican Party when I was chairman of the Democratic National Committee did not blind me to the fact that it possessed in such leaders as Senator Robert A. Taft, of Ohio, Senator Arthur Vandenburg, of Michigan, and Chief Justice Charles Evans Hughes, men of highest integrity and ability. Indeed, I found former President Herbert C. Hoover to be the noblest of opponents.

During those first years of the New Deal Administration, I was amused that opposition newspapers bitterly called me a political boss. As a matter of fact, I was spending most of my time trying to find out what my bosses—ninety-six members of the national committee representing their bosses, twenty-five million Democrats—expected me to do, in order to keep my job. Everybody may think you're the man at the top of the pyramid, when actually you're the fellow at the bottom of the pile, because you have to take the responsibility for a lot of things over which you have no control.

President Roosevelt could not have instituted all the political reforms of his Administrations if his bosses—the majority of the American electorate—had not approved of them. This is why I believe that a citizen who takes no part in the making of modern laws has given up a considerable part of his freedom.

This is also why I consider a book like Mr. Charles Hurd's more important than a mere history of politics. As a White House correspondent, he witnessed the political developments; but as a reporter he also saw the atmosphere of a changing nation and the attitudes of a struggling people.

I recommend *When the New Deal Was Young and Gay* for everyone: those who were a part of that revolutionary period and those who were not; those who favor the changes that period brought and those who do not. Mr. Hurd's fascinating on-the-spot approach is at once objective and nostalgic. His book gives perspective to the past and adds to our understanding of the world today.

JAMES A. FARLEY

New York City
April, 1965.

Introduction

THIS WORK IS PRESENTED to the reader in the full consciousness that it will neither change the course of history nor affect the American political atmosphere of our century.

Franklin D. Roosevelt has been analyzed and studied as a political phenomenon exhaustively by scholars with access to immediate material, but it is as yet too early for objective appraisal of his works.

In all of the published works, however, there is lacking the homely recounting of what it was like when this "bright and shining morning star" rose on the bleak prospects of a country—and a world—hopelessly mired in failing institutions, temporarily wandering without political leadership in a wilderness of confusion, and losing faith in its inspiring precedents.

These are the footnotes to the history of the years 1933 to '36 as organized some thirty years later by one of the few reporters who consistently wrote of the Presidency in those years, culled from his notes, his recollections and researches to refresh the background.

The writer was White House correspondent for *The New York Times* from the morning of Inaugural Day, March 4, 1933, to the second Inaugural on January 20, 1937. No period in America's peacetime history embraced higher hopes, greater controversies or more startling political actions—or brought together a more contrasting clutch of personalities.

These years also were the last in which the Presidency was as yet a personal thing, with the White House staff still small enough to work within the White House offices. Government itself still was confined mostly to the Washington establishment. The press corps was small.

The President was still absolutely forbidden by the Secret Service to travel by air; jet airplanes were yet to be invented, and of course no helicopters landed on the White House lawn. Television existed exclusively in laboratories. The only broadcasting was by radio. People still read their newspapers for reports on public affairs.

In fact, the Presidency was still as personal and intimate—and as remote from the public—as it had been in the days of Theodore Roosevelt, or even of Woodrow Wilson. No President had yet talked directly by telephone to the chief executive of another country. The only private White House telephone lines were a few branches from the switchboard to special telephones, colored white, on the desks of a few key officials in Washington, or to the President's stopping places when he traveled.

Except for special occasions, and in political campaign years, no President had traveled very much, usually no more than to a vacation spot. News agencies and papers have always paid the traveling expenses of their correspondents. By 1933 only eight of these felt they could afford to keep a reporter always with the President. Before the time of F. D. Roosevelt, this coverage had been mostly for "protection" in case of mishap.

Presidents Harding, Coolidge and Hoover had transacted White House business in the White House, in an atmosphere of morning coats, white-tie dinners and candle-lit receptions. Their engagements had been well spaced, and afternoons leisurely. Even in the crisis of the Depression, a small corps of secretaries and an efficient mail room, supplemented at the most by weekly Cabinet meetings, had carried out White House chores.

Press conferences in the Rooseveltian sense were unknown. Formerly at these infrequent gatherings, Presidents would receive questions written out in advance, reply if they chose, and seldom enlarge upon those replies prepared in advance.

In the interval between the election in November of 1932 and Roosevelt's Inaugural on March 4, 1933, the White House pace and its echo in news slowed even more. This "lame duck" period of Federal Government, when a defeated President as well as many rejected congressmen still ruled, was two months longer in 1933 than it is now. (Before the 1937 Inaugural, a Constitutional Amendment set the date back to January 20.) The length of time accentuated defeat and bred inactivity.

By contrast, the incoming Administration turned into a tornado of activity. As an example, at the end of F.D.R.'s first year in office, Edwin L. James, managing editor of *The Times,* laconically commented that the paper had printed one million words of Presidential stories, issued technically from the White House but more often from points outside of Washington. Many front-page stories were filed from the President's train, others written literally on reporters' laps in speeding automobiles, and still others from datelines never before in print.

The White House was where the President *was,* and he might be—many times was—at Hyde Park, Warm

Springs, Campobello, even offshore sailing a schooner to which he would summon officials for a conference and aboard which he would announce vital decisions and actions.

Parallel cases in the Administrations of John F. Kennedy and Lyndon B. Johnson may make such Presidential activities seem hardly worth mentioning today; but if there were no other difference, these later Presidents could walk on the ground easily and painlessly and, by the use of airplanes, they could fly.

In the jet age, which telescopes miles so dramatically, a transcontinental journey has become a five-hour trip. On the President's special train, to which he was limited, over his protest, by those charged with his safety in the 1930s, forty miles an hour was a fair average. It required a lot of those train hours for Roosevelt to travel one hundred thousand miles in his first term alone.

Yet that was how news reporters got to know him, his family and official aides probably better than any official White House entourage will ever be known to newspapermen again.

Although great actions and events necessarily supply the background for this book, and although the electrifying changes that struck a drowsy Washington, D.C., in the 1930s are reflected here, this is primarily a story of people —of people on the move.

CHARLES HURD

New York City
February, 1965.

Contents

Illustrations

PART ONE
Chaos and Promise

The Inaugural, March 4, 1933 (*Wide World*)

CHAPTER 1

The Great
Depression

THE INAUGURATION OF FRANKLIN D. ROOSEVELT on
March 4, 1933, represented for the United States a victory
that some day may be considered far more significant than
either the country's notable victories in war or its more
recent economic and social expansion.

Not in the person of the President but in the act of
transition from the old forms to the New Deal, without
armed rebellion or dissolution of American society—re-
gardless of the bitter and sometimes tragic conflicts involved—the United States proved itself to be worthy of
its heritage and the future built from that period.

In a new generation we take recovery from the Great
Depression for granted. It sometimes seems to have been
merely an awkward moment prior to the grand history
of victory in World War II, leadership in the modern
world's affairs (possibly exaggerated), great economic
and military might, atomic development and the conquest
of space.

Today the United States still faces the challenge of its

"poverty pockets" and debates seriously the growth and future extent of government controls over individuals.

Yet all this has been done with—and could not have been done without—the new political outlook and new economic society that dims the memory of the valley out of which our country had to climb.

This perspective is as important as the recollections of persons, places and events marking the turn of the tide. Therefore, as a hint of perspective, this account begins with a reporter's recollections of what the chaos of the Depression meant to those living in its time and with a brief description of the drama of Roosevelt's Inaugural after the long "lame duck" interval.

By the time the United States went to the polls in 1932 to elect a President, the business of the country and of the world was nearly at a standstill. Millions were unemployed and had no place to turn for work. Other millions of prudent or elderly persons found their savings shrunk, their dividends dried up and their stocks and bonds almost worthless in the market.

Farmers continued to produce meat and grain, only to sell them in markets that hardly yielded the cost of production in return. Many insurance companies that held farm mortgages not only withheld foreclosure but also helped farmers to continue working in order to save the land.

It was figured that thirty-four billion dollars of security values had been drained away into thin air, since the Depression had struck with a burst of panicked selling on the Stock Exchange in 1929. Strong corporations operated on a shoestring basis. The weak failed. Some individuals and institutions who escaped draining losses turned their reserves into gold or government securities; some looked around for "bargains" in stocks to hold against the time of possible recovery. Few would invest in new enterprises.

The depression in farm prices was already aggravated by a succession of searing droughts beginning in 1927 that had turned vast areas into barren misery. These compound tragedies created the Okies and the helpless farm poor depicted in books and plays such as *Tobacco Road*. Many great farm landlords who had been attacked in the 1920s by reformers for exploitation of their tenants approached bankruptcy themselves to feed and house these sharecroppers.

The sophisticated poor turned to laugh at themselves, as an antidote to absolute despair. Popular songs of the day like "Brother, Can You Spare a Dime?" or the romantic boast "I've got five dollars" parodied the situation. The radio team of Amos 'n' Andy led the popularity parade with a show about the struggles to survive by means of one broken-down taxicab while existing only on hope and the Kingfish's great plans to make millions.

But there also were great numbers of persons not only too poor to own a radio, but also removed by endless stretches of poverty from the price of a good meal. Some of these sold apples on street corners at five cents each. Along with the other downtrodden millions, they slept in shelters established in almost every city by municipal authorities and organizations such as the Salvation Army and the Volunteers of America. The Volunteers, in fact, solicited gifts of five dollars in exchange for books of twenty coupons; each coupon when given to a down-and-outer was redeemable for "supper, bed and breakfast." One such shelter in Washington helped hundreds of the indigent each week.

Ironic in its added effect on the Depression's spread was the action of prosperous citizens—of whom there were many—who changed from big houses to more modest living quarters not only to conserve their resources but also to appear unostentatious. In the end this modesty, real or feigned, simply added to the blight of business.

Through those three years there inevitably developed a struggle between two spheres of political thought, both honestly maintained and both subjected to unjust criticism from the opposing sides. The Republican leadership in control clung to the contention that with patience "the American way" would overcome the Depression; the Democratic minority made a joke of the prediction that "prosperity is just around the corner."

There was an almost total lack, as some news correspondents frequently noted, of effort to find a middle ground of co-operation. When the election of 1930 saw the Republican leadership of the House of Representatives overturned, the new Democratic leaders thereafter devoted all of their energies—or so it seemed—to making the Presidential and Senate records look as black as possible.

Additional embitterment and disillusionment were fueled by developments abroad that pulled down the American economy even farther and made increasingly difficult any effort to reach a mutual agreement on plans for world co-operation toward recovery.

General American opinion was "fed up" with Europe less than fifteen years after the end of World War I. There were, of course, many who did not feel this way, but on the whole the annoyance was so widespread that it seemed hopeless to expect any real international co-operation in the near future.

European governments catered to mass support in their own communities by blaming the United States for the Depression. The popular viewpoint in the United States was that its former allies were a bunch of defaulting ingrates. Of course, most of these general views were wrong, but this was no time for reason.

All of the former Allies except Finland had defaulted in payments of World War I debts, already scaled down to small fractions of their face values. Russia would not even discuss the great claims held against it. At the same time, Americans remembered that in the peace settlement the United States had not asked for reparations from Germany, leaving all of these payments for its European Allies. To Americans who had entered World War I to "make the world safe for democracy," there were very few indications that anything but chaos had come out of victory.

Furthermore, the other five Great Powers—France, Germany, Great Britain, Italy and Japan—were all going through political eras that created distrust in the heart of the average American, in addition to some downright fear of the Communist menace in Russia.

France had reached an economic impasse under a succession of failing governments, and by 1932 there were growing evidences of collusive action between financiers and government officials to enrich themselves even at the expense of the country's ruin.

France's repudiation of her war debts excited heated criticism in the United States because France, despite pledges in the Versailles Treaty, had highhandedly taken over the Ruhr Valley as security for herself when Germany defaulted on reparations.

In Germany Hitler was on the rise and so entrenched in power by 1932 that there was no longer a question whether he and his Nazi Party would seize control; the only question was when.

America held Great Britain in sentimental regard, but this did little to stem criticism of her policies. She had already gone off the gold standard, which meant under-cutting American foreign trade; many Americans held British bonds on which interest payments were in arrears; she had built up "empire preference" in foreign trade; a coalition government had introduced a form of state socialism that frightened many Americans.

In Italy Mussolini and his Fascist Party and private army held dictatorial control, entrenched since 1923 and setting a pattern for Hitler. He had begun to dominate the then important financial center of Austria, which already had gone through such a period of financial corruption that in 1932 Engelbert Dollfuss, the new chancellor, had tried to set up a dictatorship backed by Mussolini. (His later murder by Nazi sympathizers was a preliminary to setting up their pro-German government.)

On the other side of the world, Japan, which had been for almost eighty years a friend of the United States, was bowing to a new military dictatorship and starting the conquest of China. It angered American business by "dumping" exports into the United States at such ridiculously low prices that no form of tariffs could equalize the competition.

At a congressional hearing on tariffs, a South Carolina manufacturer of cotton rugs and mats produced documentary evidence of an offer by a Japanese manufacturer to reproduce his line and deliver to his shipping points the replicas of his products at far less than his manufacturing costs. The South Carolina producer rejected the offer and in the Depression maintained at a loss the three hundred jobs he supplied to Americans.

The Japanese had seized in 1931 the Chinese province of Manchuria, renaming it Manchukuo and making it a Japanese satellite. In 1932 the militarists cleared the way for complete control of the country with the murder of Premier Inukai.

Now, none of these developments was the fault of President Herbert Clark Hoover or of the Republican Party. Only a stupid critic would attempt to guess what another Administration would have done in the same circumstances.

However, in the election year, national politics turned into a power struggle which used slogans that in themselves had little relation to the issues. In the midst of misery, and oftentimes despair, the Republicans pledged to restore normalcy. The Democrats clamored for reform that would sweep out the older and failing system, but made no commitment as to their plans.

Actually, the oratory had little effect. It is the tradition of most democracies that the "outs" hardly ever beat the "ins" when the country is enjoying "peace and prosperity." Conversely, no American party has survived an election in hard times, unless the threat of national security has been on the horizon.

There is an old political adage to the effect, "Administrations can't make the sun shine or prevent the rain, but if they take the benefit of the sunshine they must shoulder the blame for the storms."

After the hoopla of the national conventions and the oratory of the campaigns, the result was much the same as it would have been if never a speech had been made.

Franklin D. Roosevelt, selected as the Democratic standard bearer, won an overwhelming victory, and President Hoover was defeated.

Then the country had to face the final, intense squeeze of the Depression. A completely discredited Administration must stand still until the next Inauguration. The

incoming Democrats, led by Roosevelt, declined offers
to consult and work with the outgoing Administration
on the ground that such action might compromise their
future program.

A new panic began and its hardships were superim-
posed upon the already broken economy.

Bank runs and closings grew in number. Bankruptcies
rose. The States were hard pressed to meet the minimum
relief requirements of the needy. Soldiers' homes and
veterans' hospitals became choked with "patients" consisting primarily of Spanish-American War veterans who
could use real or imaginary illnesses to obtain bed and
board in them. Because of the lack of accurate statistics
no one knew the number of unemployed, but it rose into
the millions.

California threatened, and desisted only under the
threat of Federal court action, to close its borders to the
needy pouring out of the Southwest.

On February 14, a gasp of dismay swept through the
nation when the State of Michigan, heart of the automobile industry and barometer of the boom-and-bust fluc-
tuations of the period, by proclamation of Governor
W. A. Comstock ordered all State banks closed for eight
days. Many did not reopen.

Hungry, sullen chaos and resentment settled over the
country while it awaited the change in Administrations.
By the close of business on Friday, March 3, more than
five thousand banks had folded.

As yet, Roosevelt had not revealed his program.

F.D.R. and President Herbert Hoover, March 4, 1933 (*Wide World*)

CHAPTER 2

The Promise of Hope

THE DAWN OF THE INAUGURAL was cold and cloudy. When Roosevelt arose early to prepare for his day by starting with special services at St. John's Episcopal Church, he put on over his formal clothes a heavy fur-lined coat with an astrakhan collar, which he jokingly maintained had belonged to his father. His starting of the day at St. John's emphasized the peculiar duality of his re-entry into Washington.

It had been twelve years—years of physical and mental anguish—since last he had lived in Washington, the capital he had left as a member of one of the most discredited teams in modern history, after the debacle of the 1920 election. He was now returning in triumph.

He sat in a pew of a church from which he had been absent as long; and yet, from his former years, he ranked as a member of the vestry. As the new President, he was a "newcomer" to Washington, but as a former junior official he could be considered in this transient city a returning old-timer.

Roosevelt had left a city marked by its broad and cheerful avenues, bordered by trees and distinguished by great houses—even palaces—along Massachusetts Avenue and Sixteenth Street, always brightly illuminated after dark. They had displayed the added wealth from the business created by World War I as well as evidences of other fortunes dating from the boom after the Civil War.

But on this morning Washington presented the façade of a run-down, ill-kept and dirty city, as yet not brightened by the leaves of the elms and oaks. Most of the great mansions were closed and shuttered, showing the results of neglect. Even the owners who still might have afforded the cost of occupying them had for the most part retreated to cheerier neighborhoods and more modern houses in the suburbs—Spring Valley, Chevy Chase, Fairfax.

When Roosevelt drove to the White House, he saw that even its paint was yellowed and peeling, since annual repainting had been discontinued as a gesture of economy by the government.

Many responsible citizens in Washington and in other cities devoutly thanked God that this Inaugural fell on a Saturday, when banks, the Stock Exchange and other financial institutions were closed. No one knew what fire might start from the sparks flying off from this changing of the guard.

Some—yes, many—feared uprisings and rioting in the cities, starting in the poverty-stricken quarters or, worse, in the shanty-towns constructed of rubbish on unused land by the migrant unemployed.

The military forces brought to Washington were primarily for pomp, but General Douglas MacArthur's staff also had been carefully briefed to prepare these forces for more serious exercises, particularly if the World War I veterans—the remains of the Bonus Expeditionary Force —who had overrun many of the vacant buildings in Washington should choose the Inaugural parade as the time for a demonstration. These apprehensions were reflections of national fears rather than local Washington reactions. In the capital, because of the continuing government payroll, the basic living conditions were not as bad as elsewhere.

New York optimistically and proudly sent a huge delegation to the Inaugural, but every member of this crowd was acutely conscious that on Thursday, February 18, Governor Herbert H. Lehman had proclaimed a "bank holiday," closing all of them. In Washington itself there had been some bank closings.

Across the country, hotels and restaurants were accepting checks of none-knew-what-worth on closed banks, or I O U's from regular customers, and a few from strangers. Credit cards were still to be invented. In Washington itself, many visitors to the Inaugural paid their bills at hotels with paper of doubtful value.

As usual, there were humorous undertones in this matter of credit. The professional gamblers took no chances. The managements of the two nationally known race tracks then operating in March of 1933—at New Orleans and at Agua Caliente, Mexico—simply closed. No races. No betting.

In the harder world of business, money had become unimaginably dear. In New York, for instance, the papers reporting the Inaugural printed large advertisements by Rogers Peet, an established high-quality retailer of men's clothing. There was a sale of men's suits in two price ranges—twenty and twenty-eight dollars. New York's first-class Barbizon-Plaza advertised rooms with private bath at three dollars a day, seventeen dollars a week and sixty-eight dollars a month, with all rates including free continental breakfasts.

An important news feature of the Inaugural preliminaries was that, despite shortage of money, all available tickets to the Inaugural Ball to be held in the Washington Municipal Auditorium had been sold out in advance at the "high price" of ten dollars a couple.

The sober and bitter, but always courteous Hoover, his round face expressionless between high silk hat and high starched collar, rode with Roosevelt from the White House to the Capitol. As they approached the building, he could hear bands playing over and over again the Democratic campaign song, "Happy Days Are Here Again."

Hoover was a famous engineer, scholar, organizer of world-wide relief programs after World War I, and three-term Secretary of Commerce—and a skilled fisherman. On this ride he certainly must have recalled that in 1920 a delegation of Democratic Party leaders, including Franklin D. Roosevelt, had offered their support if he would run for the Presidency as the Democratic candidate.

Today he saw and heard the crowd cheer itself hoarse for his successor.

The crowd of one hundred thousand persons who jammed the forty-acre plot in front of the west portico of the Capitol could only be described as ecstatic. In milling confusion, they had been jockeying for places since one in the morning.

As those in the rear sought vantage places in front, they overran the trestle tables and benches set up for press coverage. Many were bruised from being pushed against the supports of the elevated platforms that held the newsreel cameras and crews.

Another five hundred thousand persons lined the street through which the Inaugural parade would pass.

Roosevelt took the oath of office from Chief Justice

Charles Evans Hughes, while his hand rested on a generations-old Dutch family Bible, a symbol of his deep-rooted colonial origins. When Roosevelt spoke, it was in an accent new to most of the crowd, accustomed to the flatter pronunciation of the prominent southern and midwestern politicians. Yet for the moment, this Hudson River aristocrat was the man of the people.

The crowd heard him say: "The only thing we have to fear is fear itself." They cheered when he promised a "new deal." They cheered even harder when Roosevelt grimly said he would ask immediately for powers such as a President would ask only in wartime. They wanted action.

Now, all of this was a promise only, but it came from a new type of personality, and a courageous man who had not panicked when, less than three weeks earlier, he had faced an attempted assassination in Miami, Florida, where one man immediately beside him was fatally wounded. (Mayor Anton Cermak, of Chicago, who was hit by a bullet intended for Roosevelt, would die of his wound the day after the Inaugural.)

One commentator wrote that this speech by Roosevelt was a "Jacksonian speech, a fighting speech."

Arthur Krock, chief Washington correspondent of *The New York Times,* gave this sober appraisal of the speech and its setting:

> Though the city was gay with flags and lively with the music of bands and cheers for the members of the Inaugural parade which followed the oath-taking, the atmosphere which followed the change of government of the United States was comparable to that which might be found in a beleaguered capital in wartime.

Later in the day, Mrs. Roosevelt commented that the cheers of the crowd that greeted her husband's announcement of imminent demands for wartime powers were, to her, a "little terrifying."

Many others were disturbed as well, for they remembered peaks in history when a few individuals who temporarily held the destinies of countries in their hands used their power in unpredictable ways.

Those who watched the public scene, whether as news reporters or as public-spirited citizens, could not erase from their minds the seemingly deadly parallel with concurrent activities in Germany, which shared the daily headlines with the Inaugural.

Germany had long been considered as the home of a stable people very much like Americans, since the German immigrants seemed to be more responsible than immigrants from other countries. There had also been a growing feeling since 1920, contributing heavily to isolationist feeling in the United States, that probably too much of the guilt for World War I had been loaded on the backs of Germans. But Hitler could not be disregarded.

The same newspapers that for a week had reported the preliminaries of this Inaugural in Washington had been heavy with dispatches forecasting the results of an election Hitler had called for March 5, the day after the Inaugural. An overwhelming victory confirming him as chancellor, and practical eclipse of even a façade of German rationalism, was a certainty.

The sober onlookers at the Washington ceremony retained their full confidence in the American system and in Roosevelt. But they wondered what would be the effect in a year or two if the Depression were not stemmed; if the power groups continued to plead with this new President to "do something."

These groups had pleaded with Roosevelt to be firm, and he had answered the request in the words of his Inaugural, but the actions were still to be outlined. And there was much resentment toward his declining to establish himself in Washington right after election and work with the Hoover Administration.

President Hoover never forgave this brush-off, and he never returned to Washington during the years that Roosevelt was President.

It took a long time for both Roosevelt's critics and friends to realize the sincerity of two paragraphs in his Inaugural speech that contained little "headline value," but substantially showed his own view of his new job.

> We face the arduous days that lie before us in the warm courage of the national unity; with the clear consciousness of seeking old and precious moral values; with the clean satisfaction that comes from the stern performance of duty by old and young alike. We aim at the assurance of a rounded and permanent national life.
>
> We do not distrust the future of essential democracy. The people of the United States have not failed. In their need they have registered a mandate that they want direct, vigorous action. They have asked for discipline and direction under leadership. They have made me the present instrument of their wishes. In the spirit of the gift I take it.

Even while the President was speaking, his advisors were listing the problems dependent on immediate action or policy decision by him. The problems were many and varied, but for simplicity political writers grouped them in the following ten general categories:

1. Restoring confidence in the banks and insofar as possible reopening those that had closed, and freeing the billions of dollars deposited with them;

2. Reforming the currency;

3. Budgeting Federal funds to help best the anticipated recovery program;

4. Reforming the national debt;

5. Finding relief for agriculture;

6. Bringing relief for the hard-pressed railroads;

7. Reforming tariffs to encourage recovery of national exports;

8. Arranging collection of at least part of the debts by Allies in World War I;

9. Developing a realistic arms program to guard against the Nazi and Communist threats;

10. Strengthening national security through firm commitments with friendly nations abroad.

The last two points carried very little weight. Heavily isolationist, the United States considered these to be very long-range problems. Were we not protected by oceans across which no foreseeable enemy could travel and mount an invasion?

As for the whole program, one irreverent observer termed it "quite a pickle barrel," with the sweet and sour all mixed up. In the domestic picture, it involved potentially great expenditures to help many types of groups as well as plans for instituting a program of economy. Abroad it meant dunning the few friends we had for payment of their debts, while urging them to show their friendliness by strengthening their armies and navies.

The Inaugural parade lasted until dark. In it marched delegations from every state. The New York group was led by Alfred E. Smith, on foot, whose right arm continuously waved his famous brown derby to the onlookers. Roosevelt reviewed the parade from a stand said to duplicate the façade of Andrew Jackson's house, the Hermitage.

While the parade progressed, his aides were already working out a schedule of conferences to begin that same evening.

The old era was ended. Whatever conclusion the New

Deal might reach in the near or distant future, it had begun.

People asked more urgently:

Who *is* Roosevelt? What is he like? What will he do?

PART TWO
Steps to Power

F.D.R.'s family, Christmas, 1932 (*Wide World*)

CHAPTER 3

The Rearing of Roosevelt

THE AUTHOR OF THE NEW DEAL was an anomaly. His background belied his political philosophy. On several occasions he laughed rather grimly at the comment that he was "a traitor to his class."

Roosevelt came from a family whose luxurious living standards were not even dented by the Depression. Some care was necessary, as was indicated by his mother in a talk with reporters in 1933, when she said that Hyde Park House really needed a new roof, but that the estimate of $100,000 for reconstruction was hardly affordable. Yet the Roosevelt houses, staffs and family routine went on as usual.

Roosevelt was a man of "family" whose ancestors had been more or less prominent in New York for two hundred years prior to his birth. He was educated in the most exclusive manner. His family was surrounded by the trappings of wealth.

By every count, he should have been logically the leader

in an ultra-conservative group, if an active participant in public life at all.

No elected President had shared such a background except his remote cousin, Theodore Roosevelt. But in this comparison, remember that "Teddy" was not at first elected a President. He was an assertive war hero in a reform movement in New York Republican politics who was nominated for the Vice-Presidency in 1900 to get him out of the way of the professionals. Only the assassination of a President gave him his chance. Franklin D. was at that time just growing out of his teens.

F.D.R.'s family had established itself in the conservative tradition: by making money; assuming dignified and occasional community leadership; making large philanthropic gifts; carefully intermarrying into equally well-established, related families; and holding distinguished offices in the aristocratic, not the elective, tradition. The second-generation ancestor of Franklin—and of "Teddy" —was an alderman of New York from 1700 to 1712. Farther down the line, another direct ancestor was a member of the constitutional convention of New York State. Roosevelt's father's fortune automatically gave him the right to executive positions in the railroad industry but his living never depended upon office hours or titles.

In the Roosevelt family up to F.D.R.'s generation, there were no wartime heroes, no get-rich-quick speculators, and no villains. Franklin was born in the house his grandfather Isaac built in the year that James, Franklin's father, was born, 1828. There was never a break in the direct line of ancestry. The Roosevelt hardiness was reinforced by F.D.R.'s mother, who would die only in 1941, when the President was fifty-nine years old. At his mother's death Franklin became at long last the head of his own household and owner of the family estate.

In his background, there are some of the elements of his drive for power, his complete freedom to make or ruin his personal career without worry over the financial consequences to his dependents, and his seemingly utter disregard of criticism, when he thought he was right.

Conversely, there is also the development of a man "hopelessly" crippled at the most crucial point of his career, the expression of an intense love for his fellow cripples that fathered a national enterprise in itself, and a stubborn will-to-do that propelled him in a wheel chair to the Presidency.

The mists of time, obscuring the details of political history, are closing rapidly over these aspects of Roosevelt. But lacking any of them, he might not have stood before the nation in the Inaugural of 1933.

If he did lead the country back from the edge of darkness in the Great Depression, it seemed more than ever likely that he also was fighting his own way from the crippling shadows into the light of self-fulfillment.

Roosevelt was born on January 30, 1882, at Hyde Park House, situated on the east bank of a bend in the Hudson River known locally as Krum Elbow. His father was fifty years old, retired and married for two years to his second wife, the twenty-eight-year-old Sara Delano. When she became Franklin's mother she had a stepson and a stepdaughter who were approximately her own age. Sara Delano came from New England stock who it was claimed had settled in America before the Roosevelts, but the margin was narrow.

The family line was founded in America by Claes Martinszen van Rosenvelt, who emigrated from Het Rosen Velt, Holland, about 1638. Twenty years later Claes fathered a son, Nicholas, who prospered in the fur trade and changed the name to Roosevelt. He was the New York alderman in 1700. Nicholas had two sons, Johannes, born in 1669, and Jacobus, born in 1692. Johannes established the family branch from which Theodore Roosevelt was directly descended, and Jacobus was the great-grandfather of Franklin D.

There was not a trace of political activity in either branch of the family until Theodore's time and Franklin's emergence in the twentieth century, except that an ancestor of "Teddy" was one of the founders of the Union Club, a rendezvous for leading Republicans in the mid-nineteenth century. This line also helped to endow the American Museum of Natural History, to which "Teddy" as a big-game hunter later contributed so generously.

Franklin D.'s grandfather and father were registered as Democrats in Dutchess County but were inactive politically, or at least did not seek public office. The grandfather left the bequest with which was established the famous Roosevelt Hospital in New York City.

Here in every branch of the Roosevelt family tree were evidences of solid, conservative and public-spirited prosperity securely established long before the Astors and Vanderbilts became notable for their larger fortunes— and before members of these two families became neighbors of the Roosevelts on the Hudson River. Hyde Park House remained a symbol of stability for the Roosevelts throughout the years.

On a misty morning in the early summer of 1933, most of the eight reporters then assigned to travel with President Roosevelt had their first glimpse of Hyde Park House.

In the following years of the assignment, they would develop the background impressions of this unique President. Privileged to be among those eight reporters, I listened and watched intently.

Roosevelt had decided to break his galloping Washington routine with a brief visit to his ancestral home—that it was ancestral most properly and dramatically illustrated the first break with the past of the recent Presidents.

A short automobile ride from the train that had carried the President and his party overnight from Washington, around Poughkeepsie and north on the Albany Post Road, brought the party to two commonplace stone pillars that marked the entrance to a private road leading westward toward the Hudson River. Beside the entrance was a new sentry house, freshly painted, for the use of Secret Service and State Police personnel who would afterward always be on duty there when the President was at Hyde Park.

Some reporters remembered other trips to the homes of Presidents, but none was like this, neither Coolidge's comfortable but simple house at Northampton, Massachusetts, nor Hoover's large and beautiful residence on the campus of Stanford University.

This was a mellow house. Its stone façade was faded, the trees were tall, and the lawns beautifully kept. Fields to the right and left of the long driveway were cultivated partly for neatness and partly to provide feed for the riding horses that had replaced the former carriage horses in the stables. (Those fields flanking the drive had figured in an aerial photograph, published by an inimical newspaper during the recent campaign, and sarcastically captioned, "The polo grounds at Hyde Park.")

The first glimpse of the house presented an impressive view of the sweeping center section, with a portico extending over the curving graveled driveway. A closer look revealed the two large wings which had been added after the President's father had married for the second time.

George Durno, one of correspondents, whistled and remarked, "The President must feel he's slumming when he has to live in the White House."

On the portico awaiting the President was the sturdy and handsome Sara. With her was the President's half sister, almost his mother's age. Her name was often confused with Eleanor's because, after marrying still another Roosevelt, she too became Mrs. Roosevelt Roosevelt. She lived on a nearby estate south of Hyde Park House.

The President's house was by no means as imposing as the late William Vanderbilt's estate, located north of Hyde Park on the river and by 1933 a public park opened to visitors. It was less imposing than the closer home of Vincent Astor, but it was solid and opulent. Flanking the house and first glimpsed through the trees were stables, greenhouses and outbuildings. Beautifully kept terraces sloped from the house toward the river, bathed in early morning mist. Here one saw no traces of the relative poverty of the Depression which had brought decay and abandonment to so many similar houses.

As the reporters came to know this house better, so they would develop a better understanding of the man. Roosevelt's family background would also become increasingly familiar to them through visits to Campobello and, on rare occasions, to a house in the East Sixties of New York. It was Sara Delano Roosevelt who planned the New York house and constructed it in the year Roosevelt was married: a twin house for herself and her son's anticipated family, with common foyer, parlors and formal dining room on the main floor, but completely separated upper floors.

But the first view of Hyde Park was an impressive introduction to a phase of Franklin Roosevelt the country had known very little about—an introduction to the elements of the past that had made him the man who accepted the people's mandate in 1932.

Here he had been born in 1882. Here he had been tutored instead of sent away to school as a child, until at the age of fourteen he had been enrolled in Groton School to prepare for Harvard. From here he had first driven out to surrounding communities to make his first bid for political power in 1910. But by then he was no rural aristocrat, as his father and grandfather had tried to be.

Under Sara Roosevelt's guidance he was by 1910 an educated gentleman, somewhat Edwardian in his vanities, a lawyer well acquainted with his political contemporaries, and the father of a rapidly growing family, with a wife already noted for her social and welfare work.

Roosevelt's ancestors gave him a famous name and background, but it was Sara Delano who contributed the fire, the personality, additional fortune and almost masculine drive that would either ruin a young man as a "mama's boy" or fire him with extraordinary ambition.

Sara Delano's dowry was a considerable fortune won by her family in the China Clipper trade. She was proud and aggressive.

Although she went to a house occupied by her husband's first wife, she took it over. Her first step was to add the wings, turning a merely comfortable, rectangular house into an imposing mansion.

When James Roosevelt died in 1900, she was long established as head of the family. Her one focus of interest was her eighteen-year-old son Franklin. He was to continue as her central concern during the forty-one years of her widowhood; her affection and domination spread equally over his own marriage and brood of five children.

Hyde Park House became filled with mementos of

Franklin: pictures of him in polo clothes and in the blazer of the Hasty Pudding Club, scenes of his playing tennis and enjoying the activities as a member of the Alpha Delta Phi fraternity.

In Roosevelt's undergraduate years, Harvard was divided into two worlds: there were the "boys" who worked for an education, walking daily from Boston to Cambridge, or living in local rooming houses; there were the others who "attended" Harvard while living in their own flats along the "Gold Coast," with swimming pools, dining clubs and champagne parties. Roosevelt was one of the latter, but he also became an outstanding scholar. He was graduated with honors in 1904, at the age of twenty-two.

In the summers, he had been taken abroad almost every year from the age of three. He knew Edwardian social life as well as he knew the social life of New York and Boston.

Remote but closely knit relatives in England formed part of his family background. One of these, Arthur Murray, titled "the Honorable" because of his position as heir to the childless Viscount Elibank, was a very close friend. Murray already had a foot in politics as a member of the Liberal Party, competing with Winston Churchill, the rising star of the Tories. In later years, by 1914, Murray was Parliamentary Secretary to Lord Gray of Fallondon, the British Foreign Minister. Perhaps a lifelong correspondence with Murray helped to spur Roosevelt's political interests.

Roosevelt left Harvard only to enroll in the law school of Columbia University in the fall of 1904. A year later, with his mother's assent if not by her arrangement, he married his cousin Eleanor, on March 17, 1905, but, except for a honeymoon trip around the world, he continued his law studies.

On graduation from Columbia, Roosevelt took a clerk-
ship in the firm of Carter, Ledyard and Milburn, of New
York. Soon after, with his mother's backing, he established his own law firm, but almost immediately gave
up full-time practice to devote more and more time to
politics.

F.D.R., 1916 (*Harris and Ewing*)

CHAPTER 4

The Political Apprenticeship

IN 1910 ROOSEVELT was twenty-eight years old. He was identified as a Democrat and—by his own later description—a "poor little rich boy who wanted to do something constructive."

Perhaps the political bug had bitten him harder than he realized. As a young man he had seen something of politics in the higher reaches of Washington. He had visited Washington often, as a guest of the White House, when he and his wife called on her uncle, President Theodore Roosevelt. By the nature of his other family connections, he enjoyed friendships with a wide range of "gentlemen in politics."

On visits to New York from Hyde Park, and while living in New York City in the twin townhouse Mrs. Sara had built, he cultivated a wide range of friends in New York politics.

Among these was a rough-spoken, cigar-chewing, ambitious man nine years his senior who already was attracting attention when Roosevelt met him. This man was Alfred

E. Smith, a power in Tammany Hall, former sheriff of New York, and member of the State Assembly.

After meeting him, Roosevelt listened for hours to the loquacious Smith's ideas for reform and enlargement of the New York Democratic Party and plans for capture of control of the Albany legislature.

Smith's background was the antithesis of Roosevelt's. In his earlier years he had fought his way to position from the depths of the slums in New York's notorious Lower East Side. He had been successively truckman's helper, fish peddler and shipping clerk. Later he won recognition as a "go-getter" among local Tammany bosses.

Under the patronage system of those days, he finally was placed in a position of affluence by a very simple step. As recounted in his autobiography, Smith was given the post of sheriff at a time when the man in this position received fees for running his office. In a perfectly legal manner, Smith was able to save eighty thousand dollars from his income in three years in the sheriff's office.

Smith and Roosevelt formed a close alliance that lasted for a quarter century—one that close friends often questioned as to its depth—until it was broken when the junior ran ahead of the senior and won the big political prize.

However, in 1910, Smith was floor leader of the Democrats in the Assembly, and in line for the top position if control could be taken away from the Republicans. Roosevelt decided to try for the Senate seat from the district embracing his own Dutchess County and the adjoining Columbia and Putnam Counties.

On the dope sheets, Roosevelt was not given even a long-shot chance of winning. His State Senate district was overwhelmingly Republican. The word *Democrat* in this conservative rural community was synonymous with the sins of the city Tammany organization. Yet Roosevelt, remembered as wearing impeccably English-tailored clothes, with high cloth-topped button shoes, plunged into his campaign and rang almost every doorbell in the sprawling district, asking for voters' support.

There was something special about this political year, one that found New York State's voters as irritated with the Republican leadership in Albany as they had been annoyed with Tammany Hall. The Democrats gained control of the legislature in a landslide. Roosevelt won the State Senate seat and Al Smith became leader of the Assembly Democratic majority.

Immediately Roosevelt became a maverick in the Senate by organizing a small but intensive fight that burst into national attention and won first the opposition but then the admiration of Smith. Roosevelt took on as his opponent Charles F. Murphy, boss of Tammany Hall.

At this time, and for the last under New York laws, members of the United States Senate were chosen, not by popular vote but by a majority vote of the combined membership of the State Senate and the Assembly, in which Tammany held Democratic control—or so Murphy thought.

When the new Assembly met in January of 1911, the Democratic candidate to replace retiring Republican Senator Chauncey M. Depew was a character named William F. ("Blue-Eyed Billy") Sheehan, protégé of Murphy and friend of Smith.

Roosevelt organized a little group of about a dozen members who announced that they would not bolt their party but would never vote for "Blue-Eyed Billy."

With these votes, the Democrats could not elect their candidate. Through a three-month struggle that kept the legislature deadlocked and its fretting members in Albany, the rebels held out. Sixty-three ballots were taken without either side getting a clear majority. At last both

the Democrats and Republicans surrendered to the brash young man from Hyde Park, ditched their candidates, and agreed to a compromise on James A. O'Gorman. To a certain extent, the publicity from this fight made Roosevelt a national figure. It seemed to justify the faith his own district had in him; in 1912, when an illness prevented his making an active campaign for re-election to the State Senate, he won by a large majority. But by then he had other fish to fry.

Washington was calling to him in 1912, another year in which Roosevelt's political fortunes moved ahead over the wreckage of other shattered political empires; this time he was moving ahead nationally instead of only statewide.

The year 1912 was the "year of the Bull Moose." William Howard Taft was nominated for the Presidency by the Republicans for a second term. His first term had followed "Teddy" Roosevelt's two terms—one inherited and one elected. In the beginning Taft had "Teddy's" blessing, but it had changed to condemnation long before 1912. Meanwhile Woodrow Wilson was nominated by the Democrats at a time when the odds seemed greatly against victory—so slim that the national Democratic Party turned from its old pros to the former professor, scholar and lately Governor of New Jersey.

Then "Teddy" formed his own Bull Moose Party and began his own campaign. He split the Republican vote so badly that Wilson was elected easily, although he did not get a majority of the popular vote. And in the shadows of that victory lurked Franklin D. Roosevelt.

Roosevelt was too junior in New York, and too much at odds with the State Democratic leaders, to be a delegate to the Democratic Convention at Baltimore where Wilson was nominated. He attended the convention as a visitor, working for Wilson. His work was remembered, particularly when Wilson, assembling his "official family" prior to his Inauguration, wished a prominent New York "name" not connected with Tammany.

Perhaps with a subconscious sense of humor, he named Franklin D. Roosevelt to the secondary position of Assistant Secretary of the Navy; the same position in which Theodore Roosevelt had entered Washington official life.

With their young family, then consisting of three children, F. D. and Eleanor Roosevelt moved to Washington for a continuous eight-year residence.

Perhaps to chill the ambitions of this "upstart" the New York Democrats did not nominate Roosevelt in 1914 when he ran in the Democratic primaries for the Democratic nomination for United States Senator. The organized Democrats chose James W. Gerard instead, an older man who subsequently lost the election.

It may fairly be counted as "Roosevelt luck" that as war began in Europe and eventually involved the United States he held probably a more conspicuous post than he would have occupied in a Senate seat as a junior member.

The Navy gave the young official a romantic and headline-provoking background. At this period, too, it was prestigious to be an Assistant Secretary of any Department.

Roosevelt's chief, Josephus Daniels, was an amiable but not aggressive man, who concentrated on policy rather than action (he made the Navy "dry"). To Roosevelt was left the routine of civilian operation, including the vast construction program, speech-making and appearances before Congressional committees. Elderly men of power in the government, like the veteran Claude Swanson, chairman of the Senate Naval Affairs Committee, learned to appreciate him.

The news reports of his years in the Navy contain no

noticeable criticism of the young Assistant Secretary's
political activity in his office. To the contrary, there were
frequent compliments paid him for staying on his essential "routine" job, rather than emulating his remote
cousin who in the Spanish-American War resigned from
the same desk to brandish a saber as Colonel "Teddy"
Roosevelt of the Rough Riders.

Furthermore, F.D.R. kept growing in the favor of
Woodrow Wilson, and he cultivated the regard of Her-
bert Hoover, Bernard Baruch and others close to the
White House in the war effort.

For a young man (he was only thirty when he was appointed) with no other political achievement than a stint
as a State Senator, this was exceptional achievement.

"Teddy" Roosevelt, as already noted, had been nominated in 1900 for the Vice-Presidency as a means of shelv-
ing a nationally known and romantic figure who had been
judged by the conservative leaders of the Republican
Party as too advanced and liberal. F.D.R. had followed
in the same steps as his remote cousin, and in 1920 the
Democratic Convention nominated him for the Vice-
Presidency, to run with Governor Cox of Ohio at the
head of the ticket. The reason for the choice was quite
different from the attempted burying of "Teddy": the
Convention was seeking a young, conservative easterner
of reputation.

Roosevelt returned the compliment by waging one of
the most strenuous campaigns ever fought, "carrying the
ball" while he crisscrossed the country and leaving to
the head of the ticket the quieter and more dignified appearances. It was reported that in 1920 Roosevelt made
one thousand campaign speeches, probably an exaggeration but an impressive reputation.

Then the blow fell. The election of Warren G. Harding by an overwhelming majority was certainly not a

compliment to Harding but rather a repudiation of the League of Nations idea and agreement with the appeal of the Republican slogan, "Back to Normalcy." Whatever the reason, at the age of thirty-eight, Roosevelt found himself an involuntarily retired "elder statesman," well known to a great many people, but part of a repudiated team and repudiated policy.

With five children and a good income he might well have retired to Hyde Park and lived the type of life his father and grandfather had established there. He chose otherwise.

First, Roosevelt organized a new law partnership in the firm of Emmet, Marvin and Roosevelt, of New York City. He became a vice-president, principally for business prestige, of the Fidelity and Deposit Company of Baltimore.

He also held some unpaid offices of distinction. He was elected an Overseer of Harvard, undertook a reorganization of the Boy Scouts of America, and became chairman of a committee to raise funds for the Woodrow Wilson Foundation.

What did not show immediately on the surface was a driving ambition to use every foothold to get back into politics, until the New York leadership of the Democratic Party started again to look him over. One of those most interested in the returning native, after Roosevelt's long Washington exile, was Al Smith. In the wake of the Harding landslide, the Democrats badly needed young blood for the long, future struggle to reorient the Party.

Roosevelt's adjustment to private life and his reconstruction of political fences in New York was completed insofar as possible for the time being by the early summer of 1921. It was the first such season in years that he could plan a long vacation with his family.

The cottage at Campobello, New Brunswick, was wait-

ing, ready as always under the efficient supervision of
Sara Delano Roosevelt. Mrs. F. D. Roosevelt adjusted
her own busy schedules of lectures and appearances to devote all of her time to her husband and children. The
entire family moved to Campobello.

Summer is a short season in the far northeastern reaches
of the United States, where the State of Maine fishing
village of Eastport faces Campobello Island, across a few
miles of water. There is a great deal of rain and fog.

The water always remains cold because the North Atlantic tides sweep into the Bay of Fundy at such a rate
that they crest as high as thirty feet or more.

But there are dazzlingly lovely days as well. One of
these came to Campobello on an August afternoon.

The Roosevelt family packed picnic hampers. Led by
their tall, athletic father and their slim, lissome mother,
the children scampered down a path worn into the face of
a low cliff from the cottage to the small, narrow beach.
Immediately Roosevelt and the older boys set off for a
sail on the choppy waters. They spent several hours in the
warm sun.

They returned before the usual "flattening" of the
breeze that occurs at about four in the afternoon, to find
the picnic spread and waiting. After eating, rushing to
avoid the chill of the air that came with sunset, Roosevelt
went for a swim.

That night he suffered a chill and other symptoms of an
oncoming cold. This annoyed him, but no more than usual,
as all of his life he had been susceptible to colds. But the
next day his condition worsened, and he developed an
alarming temperature. A doctor was summoned from the
mainland.

Soon other specialists were summoned, and these men

eventually delivered a verdict that they themselves could hardly believe to be accurate.

The diagnosis was that Roosevelt—in a family without such a precedent, at an unlikely age and in a region that had not been invaded by this epidemic—had developed a case of the great and mysterious poliomyelitis. Why? How? None could guess.

Actually no one knew anything about the disease, except its effects. It was as mysterious to "modern" medicine in 1921 as the plague had been to people in the seventeenth century. It struck without apparent cause. No one knew whether it was contagious, although in rare instances there were duplicate attacks in families. There was no specific treatment for it except rest and sedatives to ease the initial pains.

If polio settled in the vital organs, paralyzing the functioning of brain, heart, lungs or other essential body activities, it was fatal.

Sometimes the attacks of polio exerted their worst effects only in the extremities. That was why, as a rule, those who survived polio were crippled in the arms and legs. One tragedy of the disease, which then was striking nearly 500,000 persons a year (mostly children), was that no one could see its ultimate effects until it had run its course.

For a long while, the doctors despaired of Roosevelt's recovery. They drew a kind of curtain around him to wait for the end. The children were sent home. His law firm ceased to forward briefs or reports to him. Messages of sympathy flowed to his family.

Then Roosevelt began to recover. But he slowly realized that what still lived in him was almost as bad as if he had not lived at all. He was completely paralyzed from the waist down.

There would be no more romping with the children, no more carefree holiday trips, no more long hikes and swims, no more political campaigning.

No one ever knew his thoughts as he lay in bed, undoubtedly resentful but never resigned. Neither his wife nor his mother ever discussed publicly the conversations of those days.

But there is one anecdote, perhaps apocryphal, which news correspondents heard from old Campobello residents when they traveled with Roosevelt for his first holiday as President in 1933. This was his first return since the attack.

The story was that when Roosevelt could be moved in 1921 and returned to Hyde Park a handful of old island friends were permitted to call and say good-by. They found him lying in bed, but smiling grimly. After each had said some greeting, he is said to have replied, "I won't see you again until I am President of the United States."

In the pool at Warm Springs, Georgia (*Wide World*)

CHAPTER 5

The Road Back

IN HYDE PARK HOUSE there is a small library, or office, that from boyhood was Franklin D. Roosevelt's private cubicle. Here he studied his lessons when taught as a boy by tutors, did his vacation assignments during later school and college years, and here he catalogued his stamp collection.

Even after he became President, it seemed to those around him that this was his favorite retreat. In it he had placed his prized memento of Woodrow Wilson— the desk used by Wilson aboard the liner *Washington* on his journey to the Versailles Peace Conference.

On this desk stood a large photograph in a heavy frame. It was an enlargement of a picture taken by some anonymous newspaper photographer. Caught in excellent focus and light, it showed the vigorous Assistant Secretary of the Navy marching down Fifth Avenue in New York City's Victory Parade. Roosevelt was wearing a light suit, smiling broadly, and waving a straw sailor hat.

This picture was placed on his desk in 1921 and it was

still there in its polished frame in 1933. It seemed to have become Roosevelt's symbol and challenge after the long journey by train that returned him as a cripple to Hyde Park.

From that point, Roosevelt devoted himself with dedicated energy to two objectives, and soon was to add a third which would culminate after his death in almost miraculous success. The two primary efforts were to recover his strength and to restore his political career. The third was his singlehanded establishment of the work that eventuated in the Georgia Warm Springs Foundation.

If these three goals seem ambitious or merely the dreams of an overoptimistic man, the observations of a medical authority might be helpful. Dr. Frank Hoch, a specialist in therapy who was brought in on Roosevelt's case when the disease had run its course, was to become a great authority on the restoration of polio cripples to maximum activity. He eventually stepped out of a highly profitable New York practice to contribute all of his time to studies at Warm Springs. Nearly a decade after the time of the events, Dr. Hoch, seated on the lawn at Warm Springs on a balmy Thanksgiving-week afternoon in 1933, spoke about polio with a number of reporters.

"There is a law of compensation that works with those crippled by polio," Dr. Hoch said. He talked while fifty pitifully crippled children were busy at exercises or games. All were laughing, seeming to be genuinely gay. "Look at them," he added; "not a morbidly depressed one in the lot.

"That's what I mean. No one can really explain it logically but when—if and when—a polio victim recovers, there comes not a resignation but a cheerful acceptance of the challenges of life. Each makes a challenge out of his own convalescence, a happy experience. The only thing they universally resent is being treated as cripples."

Dr. Hoch paused to point at a child in a wheel chair propelling himself over a small hill by use of his partially sound arms. His legs hung helplessly from the seat.

"Notice that no nurse or aide is running over to help with that chair," he went on. "Of course, it is being watched to avoid the chance of tipping. But that child will make a victory by doing this thing himself. It will be one more step toward proving to himself his own self-confidence. Sometimes that looks cruel, but it is nature's way. These cripples become little giants of confidence.

"Now, I don't mean to imply that they will become exceptional scholars or gifted geniuses. But they'll grow up, possibly marry within their own group of survivors, raise families and find their places in social life—some as leaders. Our job is very largely the one of teaching other people—able-bodied people—not to treat them as exceptionals or to harm their pride by pampering them."

The conversation lasted perhaps an hour.

A reporter finally asked with reference to recent months in Washington, "Are you explaining Roosevelt to us?"

"I'm just talking," Dr. Hoch replied, smiling.

As a politician, Roosevelt was active in his own way for a considerable period before many of his friends realized that he was doing anything more than convalescing.

In his work toward physical recovery, Roosevelt faithfully followed a regimen of exercises that little by little restored circulation to his legs—although little muscular strength. He gradually learned to wear braces and to walk short distances or stand for short intervals on them, with the support of canes held in his hands—and more importantly to restore the pride that came with ability "to stand upright on his feet."

For his daily exercise, his advisors installed a pool in which the buoyancy of the water made possible movement otherwise impossible, and he adapted his swimming skill easily to the use of his arms for principal movement. Soon his shoulders and arms were powerfully developed.

Automobile engineers, before the days of automatic transmissions, had developed a type of car in which a careful driver could engage the clutch, shift gears, work the throttle and use the brakes, all with his hands alone. Such a car, a Ford touring model, was procured for Roosevelt, and soon he was driving it as rapidly and as skillfully as he had driven conventional models.

However, all of these were "summer exercises" in the area of Hyde Park, where winters are cold and people are housebound for many months.

At some point it was suggested that Roosevelt visit the historic but long-neglected spa at Warm Springs, Georgia, where winters are mild and the elevation mitigates the heat of summers. In 1924, he went to the site in the sand hills near the western border of the state.

There, at Pine Mountain, mineral waters gush from springs credited with curative powers by the Indians in the presettlement days. In the past century there was a spa that flourished, but this burned and was never rebuilt. By the 1920s it had become a pleasant summer resort for a relatively small group of people, some of whom swam in pools in which the water had a remarkable buoyancy.

The area appealed to Roosevelt so much so that he bought a farm of 2,400 acres, an impressive size but rather meaningless in value in this scrub land. Then, with his mounting restless energy to satisfy, he plunged into plans and projects for reclamation, recalling many of the things he had been told by his old friend, the famous forester Gifford Pinchot. He experimented with modern forestry plantings, and bought a bull to experiment with crossbreeding of a type of cattle that could live off the natural forage and yet produce profitable beef.

Then he turned, not as a hobby but as a vital interest, to thoughts of rehabilitation for polio victims.

Roosevelt founded and incorporated in 1926 the Georgia Warm Springs Foundation, as a sanitarium to treat children in rehabilitation but mainly as a center for study by specialists who then could publish the results of their observations and so help doctors everywhere. There was no "experimentation," only the cumulative experience.

Many individuals responded to Roosevelt's appeal for help in his project. Leighton McCarthy, the Canadian financier, whose son had suffered a polio attack, gave generously. Edsel Ford contributed outdoor and indoor swimming pools for the use of patients.

As his major contribution, Roosevelt gave over his farm, reserving for personal use only a small cottage which, from its color, was prophetically named by his neighbors "the white house."

Needing always more money to make the project workable, Roosevelt finally negotiated a loan secured by insurance on his life of $100,000, on which he would pay the premiums. (In later years this policy, taken under normal conditions, would be valuable evidence in reply to critical questions as to whether he was in fit physical shape to run for the Presidency.)

When news correspondents traveling with Roosevelt first saw the Foundation in 1933, it accommodated fifty patients. However, while it became Roosevelt's primary personal interest, it was by no means an all-absorbing venture. In a quiet but nonetheless vigorous manner, he returned actively to the political field, mending fences in every direction, cultivating new friends and restoring old associations. In restrospect, it is clear that Roosevelt

—although hampered in physical movement—was almost the man-in-a-hurry that he had been earlier.

First, there were the public chores of a man who would re-establish his political image. Roosevelt took care of these by attending the Democratic National Conventions both in 1924, when he was beginning his recuperation at Warm Springs, and in 1928, when he was strongly established at Warm Springs and not yet courting an active political career.

At the two national conventions, he appeared as something of a hero—a man overcoming great handicaps—and certainly more discussed than he would have been simply as a former holder of a relatively minor office. Furthermore his crusade against Tammany a dozen years earlier was recalled in an era when reform was in the air, at least by the New York Democrats seeking to lead the party.

Roosevelt was invited to nominate Al Smith for the Presidency at the 1924 Convention. He did, but Smith lost out in that year.

Roosevelt was invited to nominate Al Smith at the 1928 convention. He did, and Smith won the nomination for the Presidency. Thereupon Roosevelt returned to Warm Springs to become a rather remote but important "voice of his party." He had no firm plans for the future but was awaiting whatever call might come—perhaps his own nomination four years hence, since many experts thought few Democrats could win in 1928.

The Democratic Convention in 1928 was held in Houston, Texas. From it Roosevelt returned to New York to look into his affairs and then went in late July to Warm Springs. In this sanctuary he planned to limit his political activity to the quiet role of advisor, but the semblance of passivity was more show than actuality.

With him constantly now were two assistants already

so skilled and experienced, and of such demonstrable loyalty, that for the remainder of their lives they would be part of the Roosevelt "family." One was Louis Mc-Henry Howe, secretary; the other was Miss Marguerite LeHand, personal secretary. Howe had been with Roosevelt since 1910, Miss LeHand ("Missy") since 1925.

Howe was, and continued to be, an enigma even to those who knew him best. He was a man whose political shrewdness and loyalty to Roosevelt defied explanation; he went with Roosevelt in 1910 at the sacrifice of a future that appeared far more promising. Moreover, when Roosevelt's political growth did give him opportunities for unlimited personal advantage he never used them.

He was a little man, almost gnomelike, thin and short and with an outsize cranium. When Roosevelt went to Albany as a tyro in 1910, some instinct drew Howe to him. Howe was already well established as a political writer and editor, highly respected by members of the State government and by his readers. He had built up a comfortable and satisfying life.

Howe had no publicly known close relatives or family —no ties whatsoever. He jettisoned his successful activities upon meeting Roosevelt and tied his life to that loyalty. In 1912, when Roosevelt was too ill to campaign for re-election to the Senate, Howe handled that campaign and was credited at the time with a large measure of its success. He went to Washington as Roosevelt's secretary in the Navy Department.

During Roosevelt's polio attack and recovery, Howe was with him too—always in the shadows but now a member of the household. His name was often mentioned as the "power behind Roosevelt," reports that Howe never confirmed, denied or discussed.

Under such circumstances, Howe might have had any opportunity he desired; men much less close to Roosevelt went on to wide fame and many made large fortunes. But in all his service Howe clung to his one job and title, "secretary."

When Roosevelt became President, Howe thus became his principal secretary and was invited as well to live in the White House as "one of the family." Possibly with a puckish sense of humor but more likely out of sincere regard Roosevelt assigned to him the Lincoln Bedroom, formerly reserved for distinguished guests. It is a huge room dominated by a massive bed specially built for the towering Lincoln.

When Howe was shown the room, he looked around it slowly and then exclaimed, "Good God!" His first request was for a cot to be moved into a dressing room of the suite, and on this he slept thereafter.

Amazing in this association was one factor so extraordinary that it should be noted. It is not gossip. Roosevelt was fastidious, almost vain in his appearance, a gentleman born and bred—but his friend Howe shunned all forms of cleanliness including baths. On rare occasions members of the household would steal and destroy some of his riper clothes and thereby force him to replace them.

"Missy" LeHand was the antithesis of Howe—tall, well groomed, almost pretty in a handsome sort of way, with a gracious manner of hiding her efficiency. She joined Roosevelt's staff, first as an assistant to Howe and then with heavy responsibilities of her own in 1925, when the Warm Springs project was getting under way and after Roosevelt had made his first reappearance in politics at the 1924 convention.

Missy first handled the dictation, then took the added work of handling much of the correspondence that overflowed from Howe's desk. Finally she was authorized to conduct much confidential correspondence on her own, particularly in affairs where Roosevelt did not wish to make commitments over his own signature.

This pair constituted the Roosevelt "team" in 1928 when he returned to Warm Springs to await the next event in his fortunes—and to concentrate on more exercises that he had been promised would lead to effective recovery of the use of his legs.

Then, everything changed. The developments are summarized here from Roosevelt's own recollections on an afternoon in November of 1933, when he and reporters stopped their cars to have ice cream cones at the drugstore in Warm Springs.

The New York State Democratic Convention had met during the first part of September in that year, a few weeks after the national party convention. The principal job of the leadership was to agree upon a candidate for Governor, then elected every two years, once in Presidential campaign years and once in between these quadrennial elections.

Roosevelt deliberately remained away. He knew that friends would honor him with a nomination, but he said he was not interested, and he meant it, for reasons of health. Ambition could wait a little longer.

However, while on a drive one day he turned into the village main street, where he was stopped by a group in front of the drugstore. Excitedly, one of them told him that Governor Smith was "calling all over" for him, and was awaiting a return call.

Many of the Warm Springs natives did not like Al Smith, either because he was an anti-prohibitionist or a Roman Catholic, or both. They were nevertheless impressed that the Governor of New York was urgently trying to reach their neighbor and leaving messages everywhere.

Roosevelt drove to his cottage and returned the call.

Courtesy required it, and friendship demanded it; he knew what the question was certain to be and was equally certain that he would refuse.

Then, Al Smith's twanging drawl came over the telephone, challenging him. Smith did not ask about his recovery or waste any time in amenities. He pointedly challenged him with the idea that if Roosevelt would support the national ticket by running for the governorship of New York State, Smith himself might win the presidential election. Roosevelt could not run out on his party by refusing. As Roosevelt said in describing the call, "Smith lowered the boom."

Roosevelt was tempted, but as they talked his gaze fell to his helpless legs, and he recalled the promise of improvement if he patiently concentrated on the therapy. And he was only forty-six years old.

But the party needed him. He agreed to stand for Governor.

When the votes were counted in November, Smith lost the race for the Presidency. He even failed to carry his own New York State, but Roosevelt, after a campaign that ended for all time his quiet life of convalescence, won the governorship.

Roosevelt won more than the position of Governor. He emerged as the strongest vote-getter of his party. The Democratic leaders, and particularly State Chairman James A. Farley, took eager notice as they began to assay the future.

With the coming of the Depression in 1929, Roosevelt's Warm Springs visits became brief, though he still observed the ritual of eating Thanksgiving Day dinner with the children. Travel by train from Albany required several days, and by now direction of Warm Springs had passed to other hands.

He regretted the sacrifice of this active association, but

larger horizons were beckoning. The election of 1930 reinforced his ambition and diminished any doubts he might have held as to the public's acceptance of a cripple as an active and vigorous leader.

In the first campaign for the governorship he had won in the face of a national Republican landslide by barely 30,000 votes, but the voters of New York State returned him to Albany in 1930 by a margin of more than 500,000 votes.

The handwriting on the wall was plain: Al Smith and other contenders in the Democratic Party might cherish their Presidential ambitions, but a new contender was running in front.

It is fairly simple, in retrospect, to see how opportunism, chance, courage and finally strategic gambit carried Roosevelt in four years from retirement to the center of the American and the world stage.

Roosevelt's Inauguration as Governor at the beginning of January in 1929 restored to the State capitol a member of an old New York family. But unlike others from his background he was not a Republican.

This Hudson River aristocrat was a Democrat who was both inheritor of the classical traditions of his party and closely tied to the "goulash" of his party through its domination by New York's Tammany Hall. Of course, Roosevelt's sponsor, Al Smith, was a leader of the Tammany "reform" element, but somehow Smith and Tammany never clashed in party councils.

After his narrow State victory in 1928 Roosevelt walked carefully the intricate paths of political association. New York City leaders got a reasonable portion of their demands from Albany, and the Smith program for the State was honored. Roosevelt followed Smith's program of relief for farmers, his advocacy of a State power authority for electrical energy developments, his plan for regulation of public utilities and his suggested provision of pensions for the needy aged.

In a very short time, however, these programs gained the Roosevelt stamp; more importantly Roosevelt replaced key Smith people with his own. As Jim Farley and Louis Howe grew more prominent, they pushed the New York City leaders farther down the line. Both were from outside the city.

When the Depression struck late in 1929, Roosevelt's task as Governor became harder, but his leadership easier. The Depression scared the public, particularly that one-tenth of the American population who were New Yorkers. It unified them behind his relief programs.

Roosevelt, therefore, was in the right place, with the proper support when his overwhelming election for a second term coincided with the national swing in this off-presidential year to so many other Democrats. That year, while New York endorsed Roosevelt, many other States elected new Democratic Governors, the House of Representatives in Washington went from Republican to Democratic control, and many senior Senators were defeated by Democrats in their states.

Of course, no miracles were made by political changes, as the Depression ground down the economy. It is not surprising that the record shows no great achievements in recovery by Roosevelt in Albany; the national policies influenced all State governments. But his political image kept growing through conferences with other State leaders, occasional public speeches, organization of "thought leaders," and dogged field work by his political deputies assigned to plan for the next presidential nominating convention of his party.

As the convention neared, another dilemma forced Roosevelt to make one of the major political decisions of his lifetime. The decision concerned Tammany Hall.

Traditionally Democrats won New York if Tammany mustered solidly behind them. If Roosevelt were to make a serious bid for the Presidency he must have Tammany support. Yet the corruption in New York City could be smelled as far away as the Pacific Coast, and the odor would cling to Roosevelt as long as he accepted Tammany's backing.

By early 1931, it was clear that he must choose either some dramatic repudiation of Tammany Hall, at the risk of losing his own State's electoral vote, or playing along with Tammany at the risk of national defeat.

After Roosevelt won the nomination, he chose the bold course of "cleaning house" in Tammany Hall, under his powers of investigation as Governor of the State.

Judge Samuel Seabury accepted the chairmanship of an investigation committee which immediately started public hearings. The climax came on September 1, 1932, well in advance of Election Day, when Mayor James J. Walker saw the flood of inquiry coming closer and closer to him. He resigned and, as though following the plot of a cheap novel, sailed with his mistress for exile in France.

The investigation thus closed on such a dramatic note that even Tammany leaders—now overly anxious to wash their hands of Walker—could not openly criticize Roosevelt. They inaugurated their own "reform movement," and closed ranks behind him.

Thereupon Roosevelt settled down to campaign for victory on the basis of public issues that had been there all along, and which eventually culminated in the New Deal.

James A. Farley, F.D.R. and Louis Howe (*Wide World*)

CHAPTER 6

The New Deal Family

FROM THE MOMENT THAT ROOSEVELT became the Democratic nominee for the Presidency he began to build his small group of personal aides into an enlarged though still compact version of the organization started with Louis Howe and "Missy" LeHand.

Most of Roosevelt's predecessors had followed an established pattern of simply enlarging their official associations to embrace their aides, their advisors and sometimes their bosses. Even the scholarly Woodrow Wilson had at his right hand the Texan Colonel Edward M. House; and the tradition-minded Calvin Coolidge kept his intimate Frank Stearns, of Boston, as an untitled confidant; but no others were identified as sharing this confidential relationship.

Had Louis Howe been Roosevelt's only intimate, his Administration would not have been unusual; but, as candidate and President, Roosevelt gave his confidence and trust to all of his secretaries, his aides and his bodyguard. He formed a second family that became, because of the length of his Presidency, a unique institution in White House history.

There would certainly be spats, jealousies and even serious arguments, some changes and deaths—as in all large families—but no vital disappointments and no betrayals.

As he started his campaign for election, Roosevelt also drew a sharp distinction between his political commitments to be handled through the Democratic National Committee and those organizational decisions he considered personal.

To his trusted friend, James A. Farley, he delegated the political organization work with no restrictions or limitations except for close liaison with Louis Howe. However, just as Roosevelt had written his own acceptance speech delivered in Chicago, so he reserved his own authority to develop and research, to write and deliver, and to determine the timing of his major speeches. In their preparation he was a glutton for detail. It was this extensive preparation which made many of his talks seem so casual; he knew so much about each subject he could comment at length upon it. Trouble arose only when he tried to interpolate new thoughts on the spur of the moment.

This passion of Roosevelt for research was the reason for the original formation of the "brain trust." It also dictated his choice of long-time staff members, who were chosen without his seeking or accepting suggestions from other political leaders. Perhaps this ignoring of politicians was due in part to his fortune in already having a Louis Howe.

Long before Roosevelt's nomination for the Presidency and largely because of his responsibilities as Governor, he had created the "brain trust." Only later was it given its imaginative sobriquet in a feature story by Leo

Kieran, Albany correspondent for *The New York Times.*

The original members were Raymond C. Moley, Rexford Guy Tugwell and Adolf A. Berle. All three were outstanding professors at Columbia University, and Harvard-educated Berle was also a lawyer in private practice. Moley actually entered the Roosevelt enclave as an expert on public law and crime in public administration; Tugwell and Berle joined him to make studies of the Depression and of the possible correctives.

Of course, in subsequent years, the term "brain trust" was enlarged generally by the President's critics to include any member of a university faculty assigned to a position which the old pros thought should go to a political appointee.

Raymond Moley had experienced his first taste of advisory work with Governor Smith and was a well-known student and professor before Roosevelt met him and enlisted his help in 1930. Even then, at the age of forty-four, Moley, already a professor of public law at Columbia University and author of many books on law, was something of a prodigy. Among his special fields, necessarily, was the municipal government of New York. Despite one attempted reform movement after another, the city government had fallen back under the same Tammany control that Roosevelt had first bucked a score of years earlier. When Roosevelt finally "cleaned house" through the investigation headed by Judge Samuel Seabury, the advice of an expert like Moley proved invaluable.

After the success of the purges, Roosevelt invited Moley to join his circle of unofficial advisors who had been enlisted to improve the laws and to examine the legal programs of the United States. News reporters assigned to Roosevelt generally felt that the influence and importance of Moley and his fellow members of the "brain trust" was exaggerated. The responsibility was always Roosevelt's, but the contributions of these advisors to the overall planning of the New Deal were great.

Just as many experts always contribute to a final draft of major presidential speeches, so the "brain trust" worked long and hard on proposals to cope with financial and agricultural problems, general New Deal concepts and legislation, and foreign policy. Moley was the director of all of these studies.

Tugwell and Berle were brought into the planning picture to study and suggest programs in two special fields: Tugwell on agriculture and Berle on big business. Berle's job was to find means of bolstering business through government assistance beyond the steps already taken by the Hoover Administration through the Reconstruction Finance Corporation.

Rexford Guy Tugwell, aged forty-one, also was a Columbia professor specializing in political science. Although the study of agricultural problems was only one of his fields, he was given this assignment with the expectation that he would become Assistant Secretary of Agriculture and policy advisor to the politically appointed Secretary.

Tugwell was credited later—possibly with too much emphasis on his personal authority—with the programs to pay farmers bonuses for not growing crops and the licensing of planting for many of the major crops in surplus. When the Department of Agriculture paid a bonus to pig farmers for not feeding to maturity seven million piglets, Tugwell was dubbed the "pig killer."

Despite the limelight that shone on him from the start, Tugwell talked little, refrained from trying to explain himself and achieved a fair degree of anonymity.

Most successful at remaining in the background was

Adolf Berle, the third and youngest "brain-truster," already very famous in legal circles. At the age of thirty-eight when he entered Roosevelt's circle, he was both a wealthy and distinguished corporate lawyer and a professor at Columbia Law School.

A favorite political target, Berle also attracted an unusual measure of curiosity, largely because he had been marked as a boy prodigy from the moment he enrolled in Harvard as a freshman at the age of fifteen and completed three degrees in six years. When he was twenty-one he had earned a B.A., M.A. and LL.B. and had started practice in Boston. After he served in the Army in World War I, Berle entered New York law practice. Of the three, only Berle shunned public office in the New Deal. His only title would be Special Counsel to the Reconstruction Finance Corporation.

Distinctly separate from the "brain trust," and personally closer to the President were the other staff members assembled during the campaign and pre-inaugural months. They would do their jobs, fight fang and claw to protect "the boss," and in turn have his entire confidence. Moreover, they would live almost as family members, although each had some private life, of course. But they would participate in many of the President's activities; they would have their turns as guests—not attendants—at White House formal affairs and out-of-Washington picnics and parties, and accompany him on his trips.

Members of the staff had different degrees of responsibility, but each was a first-name friend of F.D.R. and Mrs. Roosevelt. It took a long time for the Washington hierarchy to understand; it took some of the more jealous outsiders very little time to start gossip, which lasted many years.

From the start "Missy" was a prime target for such gossip, since she was present wherever Roosevelt lived or worked. But she numbered Mrs. Roosevelt among her closest friends.

As Roosevelt came closer to the office of President, two other women joined his circle in a separate category from the other secretarial and clerical assistants.

Because "Missy's" responsibilities became constantly more demanding, Grace Tully joined her as assistant and as alternate in the grinding role of personal secretary.

Louise Hackmeister became a part of the White House family almost by accident. Whether as a whim or out of some developed appreciation for the need for better telephone communications in his day, Roosevelt created a special rank for the chief operator. As a skilled switchboard operator, Miss Hackmeister was assigned by the telephone company to manage the national telephone network set up by the Democratic National Committee during the campaign. In the subsequent period she came to know the voice of virtually every leading member of the Democratic Party and of Roosevelt's personal friends. She also developed an uncanny ability for locating them.

As a man who often disconcerted his secretaries by answering his own phone calls and by placing many himself, F.D.R. became friendly with Miss Hackmeister within days; soon he was calling her "Hackie." He directed that she take over the White House switchboard when it came under his control.

The Presidents long have had three official secretaries. As a candidate for the Presidency, F.D.R. found it convenient to anticipate this setup in his own staff, by hiring two assistants for Howe. The first, Marvin H. McIntyre, was another Roosevelt faithful, and the second, Stephen T. Early, had known him well while a news correspondent and later a representative for one of the newsreel companies.

Out of the past came McIntyre, a member of what

Roosevelt called the "cuff links" gang, the small team in the unsuccessful 1920 campaign with Cox. F.D.R. had given each of his close associates that year a pair of gold cuff links; McIntyre still wore his set. Marvin came from a newspaper career into the 1932 fray as a specialist in making and sorting out Roosevelt's appointments. He had the rare knack of being able to say "no" to importunate persons who insisted upon seeing Roosevelt, without making enemies of them; at least, if they became angry, it was at McIntyre and not at Roosevelt. McIntyre, small, wiry and graying, was both genial and a genius at the poker table.

After a life of frustration as a newspaperman, McIntyre worked for $10,000 a year—a cut in his previous earnings—because of two of the side benefits that went with his job: the White House limousine that carried him on all official errands and the setting aside of a special luncheon table for him at the Mayflower Hotel.

The second assistant to Howe and an equal in rank with McIntyre was Stephen T. Early, recruited by F.D.R. from the hectic motion picture industry to handle his press arrangements. Early was a bigger man than McIntyre, bluff and jovial, and more in the public eye. As he grew into his job he often spoke for the President, particularly in response to news inquiries. He was himself quoted frequently by the newspapers. Early guided the news output of the White House, took the blame for statements that drew bad reactions and shrugged off the perennial complaints of "news suppression" and "news manipulation."

In his private life, Early continued to be, despite decreasing opportunities to keep in practice, an outstanding amateur golfer. In three different years, playing with a scratch handicap, he won the National Press Club invitation tournament.

Quite unlike other Presidents' assistants, there never

developed either jealousy or other apparent discord between Early and McIntyre. In periods of vacation or illness, they substituted for each other; when Roosevelt traveled they alternated between riding the trains and—as Early stated—"tending the store." Unlike Louis Howe, neither lived in the White House, although they were eventually placed on a par officially with Howe. It is worth remarking that, after F.D.R. changed them on Inaugural Day from campaign assistants to White House secretaries, both shunned even otherwise harmless social engagements that might appear to compromise their jobs.

Sometimes visitors saw a silent self-effacing man lounging in the outer lobby of the Executives Offices after Roosevelt moved into the White House. With him, asleep on the floor, invariably was a huge English pit bulldog (a sort of white version of a German boxer). Thousands must have gone away under the impression that this dog was part of the President's safety program.

It was less complicated than that. The man was August (Gus) Adolph Gennerich, and the dog was his constant companion in his own bachelor quarters in the White House. In the new informality of the Executive Mansion, none of the President's "family" thought it strange that Gus should occasionally relieve his pet's lonely life by letting him see what was going on. And this was the pleasure he had given the dog at Hyde Park and at Albany.

In the same manner, Roosevelt had a special place in his heart for Gus, for whom the President's paralysis likewise created special responsibilities. He was the bodyguard and, after a fashion, probably the most trusted person around Roosevelt.

Normally the governors of New York State, since Roosevelt's period in holding that office, have a "body-

guard" whose duties are confined to attending the governor on public engagements and acting, though in a small
way, much as Secret Service attendants do for the President. When Roosevelt chose Gus to help him, however—
and Gus gave up his job as a New York City detective—
the position became unique. And his importance grew
when Roosevelt entered the White House. Gus combined
great strength, gentle manners and a gentle touch. He
proudly and instinctively created his own duties.

Everyone around Roosevelt lived in constant fear that
some mishap, however trivial for an able-bodied person,
might leave the President helpless, in peril or at the least
embarrassed. It was Gus's job to guard the President
against such mishaps. He was always on hand when the
President moved, from the time he lifted him out of bed
in the morning and helped a valet dress him until he
lifted him from a wheel chair, or helped to remove his
braces, and placed him in bed at night.

All of this work could have been done by hired specialists, but Gus volunteered for it. He valued the responsibility; it became his entire life—that and the com-
panionship of his dog.

Each of the individuals mentioned above came into the
White House through some prior association with President Roosevelt. Once there, two others joined the "family"
simply because their personalities carried them beyond the
formalities of official assignments. Once with Roosevelt
neither of the pair left him while they lived.

It long has been customary for Presidents to have a
large number of aides, the major ones coming in 1933
from the Army, Navy and Marine Corps (there was no
formal Air Force). These aides had to be officers of good
appearance and bearing; they had to have the rank of
Army colonel or Navy captain and the means to support

themselves on an assignment when their pay and allowances were totally insufficient.

The President also has the prerogative of designating a friend as White House physician and, if he wishes, giving him a military commission.

Roosevelt received the routine aides and approved them. Instead of giving the medical title to some old friend, he, as "an old Navy hand," asked that the Navy assign to him an attending physician.

The names of most of the aides in Roosevelt's early years have long since been forgotten, except for Colonel Edwin M. ("Pa") Watson, of the Army. Some observers felt that at first "Pa" was a little irked by the assignment. He was big, bluff and gregarious. He particularly disliked dressing up in a formal uniform to act as a glorified usher at receptions, which duty he disdainfully compared with his earlier active duty as a cavalry officer.

When Roosevelt was introduced to his new aide, standing stiffly at attention, the President asked, "Where did you get that nickname?"

"Sir," the colonel replied, "there were two Watsons in my class at the Point. The other was a little fellow. Our classmates called him 'Ma' and they dubbed me 'Pa.' "

"Glad you're joining us, Pa," the President told him, and from that moment there was no escape for "Pa."

Immediately the President broke down the rotational system of military assignments for his aides (except that each one, including "Pa," carried the Presidential messages to the staff of his service). One duty after another was found to keep "Pa" on hand. He even was taken by the President on cruises of Navy vessels, to his evident discomfort, and before long was in effect a civilian secretary without the title.

"Pa" Watson did try to break loose a few years later, when the United States was mobilizing for defense and eventual war. His age, record and cavalry training placed him in the category that could have led to high command.

But the President refused to release him.

Lest the Navy feel slighted at the honors paid to "Pa" Watson, Roosevelt turned the assignment of personal physician into an intimate and honored one. The new White House doctor was Commander Ross T. McIntire (not related to Marvin McIntyre) and upon designation Ross was promoted to captain. He, too, became a crony in the President's relaxed moments, and shared with his new friend "Pa" and the President a fine skill at poker.

Professionally, Dr. McIntire "read the books" for any information he thought might help him in directing the little that remained of Roosevelt's exercise therapy; he weighed the President regularly, took his pulse and blood pressure, and scolded him when he gained weight.

If Roosevelt in the early years had no Naval aide whom he placed on a par with his Army aide, he seemed to make a point of turning his health care over to the Navy. It was to the Naval hospital that he went for periodic check-ups and McIntire whom he referred to exclusively as "my doctor."

Some critics viewed this official "family" as almost akin to the inner circle of European royal courts. Others simply felt that, whenever and wherever the new President gave his friendship and trust, he did it for keeps.

The New Deal Cabinet. Seated: Dern, Hull, F.D.R., Woodin, Cummings; Standing: Wallace, Ickes, Swanson, Farley, Roper, Perkins (*Wide World*)

CHAPTER 7

The New Deal Cabinet

THE CABINET THAT ROOSEVELT CHOSE to work with him in the first flush of the New Deal was heavily salted with standard political appointees, to which he added a strong dash of pepper in the form of personally selected individuals he wanted and needed.

Had he lived to write his memoirs, the explanation of how he chose this Cabinet would have been one of the really fascinating chapters. As it is, one looks back now on an almost ludicrous combination of individuals meeting weekly in the same room.

With an overwhelming victory in the election behind him, Roosevelt owed few favors. No one political leader had delivered the last handful of votes that placed him in office. He showed from the start that the only strong debt of loyalty he felt he owed was to Farley.

Yet this "tyro" President—never a Senator or Representative or an outstanding leader until his recent years in Albany—set up a Cabinet that both satisfied the old professionals on Capitol Hill and opened the doors of government for the first time to the liberals.

There were then ten Cabinet members. Seven places were filled with conservative, old-line Democrats; the other three were filled with liberals who would be symbols of the New Deal "revolution." And, of these three, one was a woman; her appointment established a precedent in American history.

All Cabinet members were selected between Election Day in early November and the New Year, when Roosevelt first relaxed on a cruise on Vincent Astor's yacht.

Working with the "brain trust" and others like Farley, he called upon individuals to take jobs that they had not even imagined for themselves. In the case of two, at least, who had no real political claim on this loyalty, he gave them far more important positions than those to which they aspired. At the same time, he seemed to choose mediocre people for very responsible positions, since no single member of his Cabinet was truly a prominent national figure—at least, not of the stature which most Presidents had required for their officials.

Lord Bryce, the first British Ambassador to the United States and even more eminent as a historian specializing in American development, has been quoted as saying that "strong Presidents have weak Cabinets and weak Presidents have strong Cabinets." In Roosevelt's Cabinet perhaps the only member thought of as a strong choice was Cordell Hull. On the other hand, in the atmosphere of the New Deal, some of the "weak" appointments became very strong indeed, because of Roosevelt's authority behind them.

What was most noteworthy in the naming of the Cabinet was the Roosevelt ability of giving something to everybody. He divided these prestige offices among geographical representatives, men of seniority in the Democratic Party and, for the first time, spokesmen of the "radical" groups. In this distribution he did indeed show himself to be "an old pro." Not all groups or places were satisfied with his choices, but at least he could defend them.

The labor movement was represented on the Cabinet by a secretary that its leaders—accustomed to nominating their own spokesmen—despised. The Middle West found its geographical nominee to be a man of whom it had hardly heard; what was worse he was a "reformed" Republican. Yet to the general public, from whom approval was more important, Roosevelt could justify his Cabinet appointments. On the other hand, he carefully retained approval of the Old South, the traditional backbone of the Democratic Party in 1932, with disproportionate favors to their noted figures. And neither business nor the financial community could quarrel with the choices which interested them most.

Since names are quickly forgotten, and only the middle-aged remember today the celebrities of 1932 and 1933, I will list the names and briefly describe the members of the first Roosevelt Cabinet.

Listed in order of department seniority, they were as follows:

State: Cordell Hull, of Tennessee;
Treasury: William H. Woodin, of New York;
War: George H. Dern, of Utah;
Justice (Attorney General): Thomas J. Walsh, of Montana, who died before the Inaugural, and was replaced by Homer S. Cummings, of Connecticut;
Post Office: James A. Farley, of New York;
Navy: Claude A. Swanson, of Virginia;
Interior: Harold L. Ickes, of Illinois;
Agriculture: Henry A. Wallace, of Iowa;
Commerce: Daniel C. Roper, of South Carolina:

Labor: Miss Frances Perkins, of New York.

The offices of this Cabinet now look very "old-style." Far in the future would be the Department of Defense, overriding the three service departments, the Department of Air Force having been separated from Army (then called War) and Navy. And Roosevelt would be out of the picture before there would be created the Department of Health, Education and Welfare.

Three Senators were in the list of original selections, each a ranking member who resigned his Senate seat. Of these Cordell Hull was the youngest but, in the opinion of news correspondents, the most skilled in the talents of negotiation needed for the troubled field of the State Department.

In the Cabinet meetings and more intimate office conferences, Hull was counted upon to mediate between the more conservative group from which he came and the mavericks farther down the list in the Cabinet group— Ickes, Wallace and Perkins. Mediation would not be easy, because Roosevelt would push this trio to the front in the great controversies of his program and make them his real lieutenants in the "war on the Depression." None of these three had ever held an office in Washington, nor had they been well known by the political powers.

Hull was a rangy, handsome, drawling Congressman from Tennessee, sixty-two years old, and just completing his second year in the Senate. But he had spent twenty-four years up to 1931 in the rough-and-tumble of the House of Representatives, where he had written the income tax law of 1913 and the Federal inheritance tax law of 1916. Now his "hobby" was a hell-for-leather fight on high tariffs, which fitted exactly into the portion of the Roosevelt program dealing with his "good neighbor policy."

And Hull was a man of poise, a quality first developed

when he was a young man in the Spanish-American War. There his personal campaign had become a classic. Hull was sent to train in Florida, but he never actually got to Cuba. He passed the boring months by studying faithfully the refinements of the game of craps. He took back winnings of seven thousand dollars to his farm, money which he used to establish the foundation of his independence.

Money also figured in his acceptance of the job of Secretary of State, an office normally given to a fairly wealthy man because the costs so far exceeded the salary. There were no government-owned guest houses for entertaining, and the Secretary was given only a meager allowance for a few formal dinners.

Through the years in Congress, Hull and Mrs. Hull had built up a nice cotton farm in Tennessee that supported them in about the same manner that Andrew Jackson's farm had assisted Jackson. In Washington they occupied rooms in a modest hotel, but one unsuitable for a Secretary of State. To accept his new office, Hull had to make a deal for rooms in the Carlton Hotel at a nominal price in return for a promise to give his official "entertainments" there.

For the Treasury post Roosevelt had wanted Senator Carter Glass of Virginia, so senior and yet so "advanced" that he had written the Federal Reserve banking law during Wilson's Administration. But Glass, secure in the Senate and with enough free time to run his prosperous newspaper in Lynchburg, Virginia, declined.

The President turned then to a true "tycoon" of the conservative school but an ardent Roosevelt supporter. He chose William H. Woodin, head of an inherited industrial empire and since 1916 president of the American Car and Foundry Company. Short in stature, noted for his dignified bearing, Woodin almost lost his composure when

Roosevelt—always a fast draw in bestowing nicknames—
dubbed him "Wee Willie." His assignment threw him
into constant association with Senator Glass.

The Army and the Navy, due to both Depression budget cuts and the isolationist sentiment of the country, had
shrunk in stature so much that while their Secretaries
ranked high in seniority, little imagination was needed to
head them; these appointments were "sinecures."

Governor George H. Dern, of Utah, whose only claim
to military expertise stemmed from the presence in his
State of a few Indian military outposts still maintained
for patronage, was named Secretary of War.

The Navy post was turned into a pensioner's security
for Senator Swanson, of Virginia, who was seventy-one
years old when he was appointed. The new title honored
the Democrats of Virginia, and brought into the Cabinet
the once distinguished Chairman of the Senate Naval
Affairs Committee in World War I. The irony of Swanson's appointment, which newsmen were frankly told was
to make the old gentleman's remaining years comfortable,
was that he lived through six years of naval changes in
the world that added to his distinction.

Completing the southern contingent in the Cabinet
was Roper, another old political hand, one of the last of
the old school addicted to gracious living and gracious
oratory. It was said that in a long life, conscientiously
pursuing the path of patronage, he had never failed to be
on a public payroll.

Tom Walsh, first designated as Attorney General, had
been counted upon to give the Roosevelt Administration
a badge of absolute integrity and enlightened conservatism
in the conduct of legal affairs. Although Walsh was
seventy-two years old, he was vigorous and one of the
country's ablest investigation lawyers. On his record was
the investigation of the Teapot Dome scandals which

had involved the handling of government-owned reserves that had rocked the Harding Administration. However, Walsh overestimated his physical reserves. A long-time widower, he married again and died of a heart attack on his honeymoon.

Thus Homer S. Cummings, of Connecticut, another senior lawyer but never a holder of political office, was chosen to replace Walsh. His immediate task was to supervise preparation of the defenses against the inevitable attacks which the New Deal legislation would draw.

To illustrate finally and most graphically the traditionalism in which Roosevelt cloaked his revolutionary program, James A. Farley, the Democratic political chief, was appointed Postmaster General. The practice of choosing a political figure for Postmaster General dated from a time prior to the civil service control of postmasters. In that period all post office jobs were politically appointed. They constituted the largest single block of officeholders on the public payroll, and their jobs were at stake in every presidential election.

Farley had never held public office. Instead, he had "worked his way up" through committees and organization affairs in the Democratic Party while building up a successful building-supply business.

Even before taking office, he set up a political fortress in Washington in the Mayflower Hotel, with part of a floor for the Democratic National Committee, and the "presidential suite" for his own residence. This was the other power center of the New Deal, second in importance to, but more active in detail than, the White House Executive Offices.

These seven of the ten-member Cabinet have passed into history and have been largely forgotten. In the New Deal they were important more for what they were than for what they did—with the one exception of Cordell Hull.

The names and background illustrate the political skill which Roosevelt used to lay a foundation of tradition in his first Cabinet. The conservative appearance helped the rapid evolution, if not revolution, of his recovery program.

Most individuals in 1933, or at least those to whom news correspondents talked, looked hopefully to the new President to restore in some form the "good old days": to make the currency sound, balance the budget, encourage business confidence, reduce unemployment, placate labor to the point where it would not be troublesome—in other words, to steer the country along a path to recovery. Such dreams were built on hopes that the New Deal would provide a magic formula to reduce government expenditures, cut taxes and by "freeing the economy" encourage a new surge of prosperity.

To win maximum support from these dreamers, Roosevelt gave them figureheads who represented the conservative type of thinking they entertained, while his own projects were maturing. Such maneuvering is considered fair game in politics, and Roosevelt's plan was as obvious as anything could be in 1933, though few people chose to believe it.

During the pre-Inaugural period, Roosevelt was preparing for his real program by the appointment of the three least-known members of his Cabinet—the "action" trio who would carry out the New Deal programs being outlined by the "brain trust" and other advisors. One of the puzzles never completely solved was Roosevelt's choice of two of these three, Ickes and Wallace. He had never met either before his election, and he might have found others of equal competence among those closer to him. Neither offered extraordinary background or any measurable popular support.

Ickes, fifty-nine years old, with bright eyes peering questioningly at every interviewer and a face that seldom lightened in a smile, often displayed impatient petulance. He popularized a word in the English language when he later wrote a book describing himself as a "curmudgeon."

Ickes met Roosevelt late in 1932, after he had asked for an interview. His objective: to become Commissioner of Indian Affairs, in the Department of the Interior. The cause of the American Indians was one of his major concerns in a career already bristling with plans for reform. To his surprise, Ickes was chosen Secretary of the Interior.

What kind of man was Ickes? His political philosophy was a patchwork quilt in a casuistic era. Since the turn of the century, he had changed his party affiliation at least three times. He had also tried and abandoned two early careers and after making a prosperous marriage had become a full-time professional reformer.

Ickes already was out of college and a newspaper reporter in 1897, but he broke his career to go into the Spanish-American War as a member of "Teddy" Roosevelt's Rough Riders. After returning to Chicago he attended law school, earned a degree in 1907 and set up a practice. However, like F. D. Roosevelt in New York, he was more interested in political movements than in the routine practice of law. In 1912, Ickes campaigned for "Teddy" Roosevelt on the Bull Moose ticket, bolting the traditional Republican Party. But in 1916 he again became an active Republican and worked for the election of Hughes in opposition to a second term for Wilson.

Two defeats of his chosen leaders left Ickes in the backwash of political life, even though his horizons had been narrow. Finally he plumped for Franklin D. Roosevelt in 1932 and picked a winner at a very auspicious time. Although Roosevelt was a Democrat elected mainly by Democrats, his towering victory was supported also by liberals, and finally Ickes was recognized in the Middle West as a leading liberal.

Furthermore, in the Democratic leadership in the larger cities of the Middle West there were few bosses with whom Roosevelt wished the New Deal to be associated publicly in Washington. So Ickes was tapped for Secretary of the Interior.

Henry A. Wallace, like Ickes, had not known Roosevelt prior to 1932, but was both an important name and a symbol of reform in the agricultural picture. He was a combination of Iowa farmer, political intellectual, son of a former Secretary of Agriculture, and inheritor of *Wallace's Farmer,* a distinguished agricultural paper published in Des Moines.

Wallace already had made his own bid for scientific fame by developing hybrid corn seed that greatly increased yields at lowered production costs.

In a period when agriculture fell to such low price levels that hogs, nature's factory for turning corn into meat, sold for less than the cost of their feed, all agricultural leaders were for the New Deal, and Henry Wallace was one of their most prominent spokesmen.

It was reported that Rexford Tugwell suggested that Roosevelt interview Wallace on his ideas for agricultural reform. Whether this was the true genesis of their first meeting is relatively unimportant. To his own great surprise, Wallace was offered the post of Secretary of Agriculture and accepted it.

Finally, as "low man on the totem pole" in rank, was

the woman who among her fellow Cabinet members was perhaps best known to Roosevelt, and who was his hand-picked choice as Secretary of Labor.

Miss Frances Perkins was the first woman to be named to a President's Cabinet. When her name was announced it was greeted by almost unanimous scorn by leaders of labor, business and politics. Labor had not been asked to approve the choice, which normally would have gone to their nominee. Business leaders feared "meddling" in their relationships with labor, or a "coddling" of labor. Political leaders saw this as another invasion of their patronage rights, and disliked having three Cabinet posts go to New Yorkers.

Cartoonists delighted in caricaturing Miss Perkins. They cruelly emphasized her plain features and the tri-corn-shaped hat which, made in different materials, she habitually wore.

But these critics had not, for the most part, seen Miss Perkins in action in New York and did not know her well —her skill at repartee, her scornful replies to vapid criticism, or her intellectual preparation for her job. Unfortunately her sense of humor under fire was not very great. But she had the qualities that Roosevelt was seeking, and the nerve to face her critics. She was more seasoned in politics than many of them realized, or than many of them were themselves.

A graduate of Mt. Holyoke College with a Master of Arts from Columbia University, this small, determined woman become a potent lobbyist in Albany. She was credited with leadership in forcing through the New York Legislature revolutionary laws governing safety in factories and maximum-work-hour laws for women. In those days such activities were considered dangerous radicalism by conservatives.

However, Al Smith respected her, and she grew in the

regard of the reform Democrats. When Roosevelt became Governor he made Miss Perkins a member of the
New York State Industrial Board and placed in her
charge the enforcement of the State's factory and labor
laws.

Such was Roosevelt's first Cabinet, sworn into office on
the evening of Inauguration Day.

Even the induction was symbolic.

At noon on that historic day, Roosevelt had taken
the oath from Chief Justice Hughes, symbol of all that
was great in the conservatism of the American past. But
for administering the oaths of office to his Cabinet, he
invited to the White House a Jew and open liberal, Louis
Dembitz Brandeis, formerly a crusading lawyer.

PART THREE
Political Revolution

F.D.R. and Cordell Hull (*Wide World*)

CHAPTER 8

Crash Program

AFTER THE LAST BAND had passed the White House reviewing stand, after the Governors who had come to Washington had been received and refreshed with glasses of punch and finger sandwiches, and after the Cabinet had been sworn into office, the New Deal began operating immediately.

Gathering in prearranged groups, the President's "brain trust," his Cabinet aides and key members of Congress prepared then and there for a hard night. There was no leisurely departing for home; the men opened their brief cases and went to work. The focus of their attention was the bank crisis—the five thousand already closed and the twelve thousand whose officers wondered what would happen when they opened for business on the following Monday morning.

While the conferences went on, and the President conferred with them in groups, staff aides brought in periodic reports of reaction to the Inaugural Address as reported on the radio that evening. Later came digests of reaction printed in the early editions of the Sunday newspapers.

On the whole the reaction to the President's first words

was good. The speculations concerned the possible actions that would follow the spoken words.

Finally the great decision was taken—a decision for which it was agreed there was no practical alternative. A proclamation was prepared for delivery on the following morning (Sunday, March 5), declaring a bank holiday effective from Monday through Thursday (March 9), on which day the new Congress would be called into special emergency session.

The banks were ordered to remain closed under the somewhat questionable authority granted the President in World War I, the Wartime Act of October 6, 1917, passed for the emergency and never repealed. In the same proclamation, Roosevelt ordered the stock and commodity exchanges to remain closed.

In calling the Congress into special session he declared the intention of obtaining emergency legislation that would legalize what he had already done. He also ordered "licensing"—which meant effectively stopping—withdrawals of gold and silver from depositories. These withdrawals might have been transacted through private arrangements even though the front offices of the banks were closed.

Because of these decisions, lights burned around the clock in the offices hastily assigned to the President's own staff in the Treasury Building and in the offices of the skilled "drafting clerks" in the Capitol.

Supervising the new legislative program were expert men without whose co-operation Roosevelt could not have moved at all; their joint assistance was indicative of true unity in the government during this crisis.

Chief among them in this banking surgery was Senator Carter Glass, who had turned down the offer of the Treasury Department to remain a Senator and chairman of the Banking and Currency Committee. Handling the House of Representatives in this program was John Nance Garner, now Vice-President but, until the adjournment of Congress and the Inaugural on March 4, the Speaker of the House.

Yet even with this assistance, it seemed almost unbelievable to veteran Washington observers how fast the Congress acted on the requested laws when it met on the following Thursday. There simply was no precedent for this speedy show of approval.

Ordinarily requests by Presidents for major legislation require weeks or months for passage; so would much of the remainder of the New Deal's initial program. The steps usually involve committee hearings both in the House and Senate, long negotiations and compromises between various blocs, and finally the resolution of differences in the versions passed by each house of the Congress.

In this case the law requested by Roosevelt was passed and sent to him for approval in *seven hours* after it had been introduced.

This single law gave Roosevelt dictatorial power over credit, money issued by the government, production and purchase prices of gold and silver, and all transactions in foreign exchange. No man at the time could even define the scope of the power involved. It was the largest single peacetime grant of power ever conferred upon a President.

At the time of this emergency legislation, a commentator recalled a remark attributed to former President Coolidge: "When a man enters the Presidency, with the country wholly supporting him, he can if he wishes becomes the most powerful tyrant the world has ever known."

In fact, with passage of that law, Roosevelt faced a

test of sincerity from which he emerged with honor and no serious rebuffs—although the Administration would face many challenges about details of the bill.

During the week in which this action was taken, in the event that public reaction would not favor this tampering with money, or that legal technicalities might be thrown in the way of the program, the Federal Reserve System prepared to print "scrip" to replace money. This paper never had to be issued.

Since the government feared that those who held gold would hoard it, hoarding was declared illegal; and all holders of the metal were ordered to turn it into banks in exchange for currency. New currency was hastily printed, without the former promise to redeem paper money for gold or silver on request.

Within days, banks were reopening, and by March 15 the Treasury Department reported that 1,500 were doing business without further runs caused by panic. The government moved toward a promise to guarantee deposits in the reopened banks, and soon it was reported that 13,541 banks were back in business.

The stock exchanges were permitted to resume trading on May 15; and if any further indication of confidence in the government were needed, the New York Stock Exchange reported that at the close of business on that day securities showed an average increase of fifteen per cent over the quotations last registered on March 3.

Of course, all of this activity did not run with ideal smoothness. Many underworld "rings" tried to organize the bootlegging of gold abroad, where it could be exchanged for the money of other countries that still traded freely on the gold market. Large shipments were seized on New York piers. No one knew how much slipped through the embargo net.

On March 19, therefore, the President ordered an embargo specifically on all gold exports, except for the bona fide account of foreign governments, which meant actual abandonment by the United States of the gold standard.

This action did draw sharp criticism, but it was largely squelched by an endorsement from probably the greatest living authority on finance of the day, J. P. Morgan. He gave his approval, even though United States bonds fell in the world market.

The last step in abandonment of the gold standard came late in May, when special legislation canceled the "gold clause" in all public and private contracts.

Although the public tolerated and even showed confidence in this strange and hard-to-understand tinkering with money and credit, Roosevelt found that a very touchy problem had been created right on his own political doorstep. This was the "silver problem" that had plagued the government since agitation in the last century had forced it to fix high prices for silver and to buy all offered by American mines.

The "silver bloc" was a powerful group which included the spokesmen for many States; moreover, its outstanding leader was Senator Key Pittman, who had just become chairman in the new Congress of the Senate Foreign Affairs Committee. Pittman, an experienced political strategist and former speculator in Alaska and Nevada, would loyally back any element of Administration foreign policy, but he would use every stratagem he knew to protect the price of silver. Gold was less of a problem as its production was fairly limited and not interwoven with the mining of other more common and profitable metals.

Soon the government promised to continue purchasing silver and gold as before, even though it was no longer needed as money, and to store it, except for limited sales to jewelry manufacturers and other established trades. Disposition of the rest of the gold—burying it—eventually

resulted in the establishment of the fabulous vaults at
Fort Knox, Kentucky.

Thus the New Deal cleared its first critical hurdle, and
there came a little breathing spell.

Nothing had yet been done to reduce unemployment,
to spur business recovery or to streamline government.
But the slide toward the bottom had been checked. Most
of the fear had been allayed.

On March 12, the President went on the radio to talk
directly to the public in a "fireside chat." He summarized
what had been done and promised to make other reports
about the progress of the program. It was generally agreed
among observers that no man in memory had ever stood
on a higher peak of confidence with the American public.

Now all of the outer aspects of the White House were
calm and quiet, almost desolate to the casual observer
walking along Pennsylvania Avenue and peering through
the tall iron fence enclosing the front grounds. The same
deceptively quiet atmosphere extended even into the Executive Offices in the small west wing of the White House.
Even the hectic planning and law-drafting activities were
so dispersed as to make hardly a ripple on the surface of
the capital city.

News reporters began to have the time to look in on the
newly reorganized Departments, and to report staff activities by the permanent civil servants. They could note
Jim Farley's flat refusal to turn Democratic patronage in
New York State over to Al Smith and report Jim Farley's
own proposal to put all postmasters under Civil Service.

They also had to examine critical questions in foreign
affairs ranging from frantic attempts toward real disarmament to tough talking with Hitler about his treatment of Jews, even those of American citizenship.

Individuals and delegations seeking interviews with the

President were endless. All had either complaints or plans of their own. There were groups representing segments of business, committees and crowds of labor leaders, mayors from cities threatened with bankruptcy in their care of the needy, insurance company spokesmen fearful of mortgage losses that would ruin their reserves, and delegations from farm and home owners protesting against foreclosure.

During that first month, in LeMars, Iowa, a mob kidnapped a judge and threatened to hang him on the spot if he did not promise to refuse further applications for mortgage foreclosures.

Thus far the New Deal had dammed a single flood of despair, but had accomplished nothing positive. There was still the challenge of relieving the hardship in the homes of unemployed millions, of putting purchasing power into the pockets of the hopelessly idle. Plans were hastily considered to spur business revival to create profits and jobs. Plans for public works began to take shape.

Because of this planning, there dawned another inescapable conclusion, hinted at recently in the political campaign and during the interim before Roosevelt's Inaugural, but hardly ever spelled out. If the Federal Government were to take all the steps indicated, wide regulation of the economy, extensive alteration of taxes and such massive aid to oppressed communities would have to be instituted. Regulation invariably would mean imposition of controls on business, and on labor. Aid to the States and cities would mean an invasion of what had been called States rights.

There were daily conferences in the private offices of leading congressmen and in the Departments on the political impact of such changes, and of their effect on the American traditions of politics. But the demands for action outweighed the doubts—for the time being.

The government leaders thus moved rapidly from discussions of how to relieve the effects of the Depression into programs frankly designed to recast in particular ways the traditional American way of life. Proposals to regulate great sections of business, to control competition, to take steps toward establishment of minimum wages on a national scale were discussed openly.

Another major philosophy was one that individual hardship due to circumstances beyond a person's control was more than a community responsibility; that assisting the oppressed was a rightful responsibility of the Federal Government. Most revolutionary of all was the theory that when business slackens, the government should spend money—even if it has to go into debt—to "prime the pump" of the economy.

Not all the Washington leadership, or outspoken business leadership, agreed with these theses. Some critical comparisons were made with various European countries which had already adopted these "socialistic schemes." But the planning went forward and drafts of new laws flowed to Capitol Hill. Under Roosevelt the White House became a power center of unprecedented proportions from that time on.

At first, only a few new faces were exposed to the public eye, by announcements in newspapers of their appointments in the new structure. On March 6, Moley and Tugwell were named officially to their promised posts, but this action was little more than a formality.

Significant among the new appointments was that of Lewis W. Douglas as Director of the Budget, a position which Roosevelt simultaneously announced would rank with membership in the Cabinet.

Douglas himself was a kind of "brain truster," although his academic years as a teacher of history at Amherst were well in the past. More recently he had been a member of the House of Representatives and, in private life, manager of a huge family fortune built on copper interests accumulated by his father. He accepted the appointment thinking he would preside over retrenchment and reduction of the expenses of the government, thus precipitating the first important misunderstanding to upset the higher echelons of the New Deal.

Before the end of March, 1933, the historic "hundred days" marking the opening of the New Deal were under way. Now, as they entered a less hectic period—and Roosevelt could turn attention to foreign affairs almost as pressing as domestic problems—an opportunity came to look around and see the make-up of the power center in 1933.

Raymond Moley, Rex Tugwell, William H. Woodin
and F.D.R. (*Wide World*)

CHAPTER 9

Power Center

HEADQUARTERS OF THE POWER CENTER in Washington, the President's Executive Office, is and was a deceptively simple and unostentatious suite. Sometimes it has been deprecatingly compared to the grandeur of offices in older palaces of the European chiefs of state.

When Franklin D. Roosevelt took office in 1933, the President's staff, numbering about 125 persons, was still housed completely in the White House office wing. These rooms were exactly as they had been designed when the office wing was added to the White House. Barely thirty years had elapsed since the President of the United States moved from the former working quarters among the bedrooms on the second floor of the White House.

Roosevelt began his Administration with a staff comparable to that employed by Hoover. He had three official secretaries, a semiofficial personal staff and the clerical career force of the White House.

His was not a highly personalized office. A few ship models, some framed photographs, and a clutter of souvenirs on the desk, including a toy donkey, were the only Roosevelt additions. The desk was a relic from the past, but not notable or old. Any need he may have had to be surrounded by personal things was satisfied by his visits to Hyde Park.

In his desk, he found a personal note from Hoover that brought with it a sentiment which transcended politics: it was a note asking that he consider helping one of Hoover's aides who had served him long and who might have trouble finding employment. Roosevelt did.

Visitors to the President found him seated at his desk, with his back to a bow window overlooking the White House lawn, and facing a traditional Colonial fireplace in which a fire glowed on cool days. Chairs and sofas lined the wall. Three doors opened into this room.

One led from Howe's office, and opposite it was a door to the personal secretary's office. A third, facing the President, provided an exit directly to the main hall through the office wing. On the opposite side of this hall was the Cabinet Room.

With the change of faces in these offices on March 4 came another change: the spectacular increase in the list of callers, from the previous three or four a day to dozens of individuals and large members of groups. The office day was divided into segments sometimes as brief as five minutes—a schedule seldom kept punctually but remarkable in that it was kept at all.

Roosevelt usually arrived at his desk, during his first hectic months in office, punctually at 9:30, wheeled in a chair from his bedroom. He began his day with a clear desk, except for a folder containing background notes about the callers' list, which was on a typed sheet mounted in a frame.

There was some critical comment, at first, about Roosevelt's apparently leisurely office hours. A few gossips recalled that Calvin Coolidge had been famous for appearing at his desk as early as 7:30 (no one quite knew why he did), and Hoover had usually started his working day at 8:00.

These people found it hard to believe, if they wanted to accept the truth, that in deference to his paralysis Roosevelt appeared in his office only after an early breakfast, an hour spent in bed reading six newspapers and clearing away memoranda and letters. This correspondence had been referred to various officials on the previous afternoon and returned to the White House during the evening or night.

Soon he increased this load of "bed work" by issuing instructions that he should also get each morning a sampling of the mail—not sorted by the staff—but as it came in miscellaneous bundles. These samples grew rather ponderous when the imminent fireside chats began, with invitations to the general public to write to him of problems. Sometimes the volume of letters reached forty thousand in one week.

Furthermore, Roosevelt became the first President to use the telephone frequently and freely for fast conferences with congressmen, official aides and outside friends. He dispensed with the more formal exchange of notes that had marked as recent an Administration as Wilson's. Wilson would tolerate only a single telephone line to his office and almost never used it. By contrast, Roosevelt initiated the practice of having special telephone lines run to a host of Washington offices, for direct and private conversation through the White House switchboard.

Thus by telephone Roosevelt ran the hectic but vital part of his Administration with his own personal network of staff and aides—Tugwell, Moley, Berle, "Tommy" Corcoran, Judge Sam Rosenman, and some Cabinet members, together with friends on Capitol Hill.

None of this activity was apparent to outsiders. The official callers representing public groups or the Miss

Cherry Pies from one State or another came through the public gate past a sentry box and on into the beautifully proportioned lobby of the office wing. Here things remained as they long had been; it was not Roosevelt's way to tamper with tradition.

Pat Simmons, retired Secret Service agent and now receptionist, greeted every caller with a courtly bow and announced him to the appointments secretary. Colonel (Kentucky variety) Edmund E. Starling, Chief of the White House Secret Service Detail since Harding's Administration, discreetly watched the flow of visitors from his office cubicle.

The newsmen and cameramen led the only *un*quiet lives in this lobby. The reporters, quartered in a small press room near the entry, lounged on sofas in the lobby between stints of news dictation, watched the callers come and buttonholed them for interviews when they left. But the most distinguished visitors seldom used this entry.

There were two other ways by which more important Presidential callers could be received. In subsequent years, Presidential security has evolved even more complicated means of receiving and sending out visitors, but the Roosevelt program was developed for the simple purpose of ensuring Presidential privacy. F.D.R. insisted upon this privacy in spite of loud protests that the President is not a private person, but a public figure. The argument still goes on today.

Personal visitors simply could be invited by special arrangement to drive into the White House grounds through one of the private gates, alight at the family entrance and be taken through private corridors to the President's office.

The most important visitors, those needing absolute privacy (who might be glimpsed using this semipublic means of entry), were taken to the State-War-Navy

Building, as though on departmental business, and were led through a damp tunnel to a White House entrance close by the President's office.

If these plans seem primitive by later standards, they illustrate the transition taking place between the older, more leisurely and less demanding days of the Presidency and the onrushing developments which foreshadowed the hectic life of the future.

In a later chapter, Roosevelt's history-making "fireside chats" will be discussed at length, but a glance at them here will help explain the transition.

The White House has today a complete television center, installed by the broadcasting networks in 1964. In 1933, the White House was not even prepared for radio; for that matter, when motion pictures were shown as entertainment, the movie distributors had to move equipment into one of the parlors, just as they had done for Woodrow Wilson.

When Roosevelt made his early radio broadcasts, and listeners were enthralled by his opening greeting, "My friends," the immediate scene resembled nothing so much as a game of play-broadcasting put together by energetic youngsters.

A basement room was partially cleared of museum pieces including mementos like the remains of the Monroe gold dinner service and other items later catalogued by Jacqueline Kennedy. Into the room was moved a dignified-looking table at which Roosevelt could sit with his head and shoulders showing above a battery of microphones. Before him was placed his manuscript. Behind him to the right and left were placed standards bearing the American and the Presidential flag.

No member of the radio audience saw these props; they were stage dressing for that other great phenomenon of the 1930s, the newsreels. Remember that people read their newspapers and listened to their radios but went to the movies on an average of twice a week to see the news.

Filming of the broadcasts required as much care as the modern production of television programs, but newsreel budgets limited producers to the use of portable equipment. Beyond the viewing limits of the cameras, the room was almost filled with their tripods, cables, sound boxes and attendant personnel. In the pre-air-conditioning days, even a short broadcast under the required intensive lights would find the President smiling and saying his "goodnight" in temperatures close to one hundred degrees. His smile was bathed in perspiration.

Then there was the less critical but nonetheless upsetting problem of serving the office luncheon conferences initiated by Roosevelt. His predecessors had followed the custom of walking over to the White House even for small and informal luncheons. Often they remained away from the office the rest of the day. Their schedules were not too heavy, and of course they could walk about at will.

So sudden was this change that the White House kitchen, large and well stocked as it was, could not serve a hot lunch at the distance separating it from the Executive Offices. In his first few days in office, all the President could offer guests was picnic fare, chicken salad, cold meats or delicatessen, no matter how beautiful the china on which it was served. It was much later that a portable steam pantry was finally provided—a prototype of the "coffee break" wagons later commonplace in modern office buildings.

To make White House life still more trying for the harassed President, there was not a single means of getting even minimal exercise. The House and Senate had already provided themselves handsomely with gymnasiums, steam rooms, rubbing rooms and all the paraphernalia of well-appointed clubs; but either political economy or simple lack of interest by earlier Presidents had excluded all such niceties from the otherwise luxurious White House.

Since Roosevelt could not take the long walks that seemed to suffice for exercise for many Presidents, or go for a drive in his own manually operated small car, he was housebound and fretful. He began to gain weight despite rigorous dieting that, in turn, seemed to create in him an added susceptibility to common colds. The lack of facilities to "keep in shape," always a fetish with him, was one reason for his early exhibited dislike of life in the White House.

Dr. McIntire was credited with making public the suggestion that brought the first Roosevelt innovation to the White House—the swimming pool that has served every President since. And he did it without intruding on the economies of the early New Deal.

The New York *Daily News*, first an ardent supporter of Roosevelt and later one of his bitterest foes, took up the project. It sponsored a campaign for penny contributions from children, as a thank-you for the March of Dimes annual campaigns waged against polio. The pool was built off the long corridor separating the main building of the White House from the offices, and swimming became the best-known Presidential indoor exercise until John F. Kennedy introduced the rocking chair.

Jim Barnes, a veteran lobbyist then in his seventies, lamented one day to cronies at the Burning Tree Club: "I hiked a thousand miles with Teddy Roosevelt, played croquet with Taft, threw around a medicine ball with the Cabinet and had to learn to play golf with Harding, and now I suppose I've got to learn to swim."

He need not have worried, for Roosevelt's swimming permitted no intrusion by outsiders, but as a result, the

President's weight declined, his humor increased, and his morale was sustained during the periods between visits to Hyde Park or occasional longer trips. But here again he was irked by the limitations of his office. He had long since flown as a passenger on airplanes, which already vied in safety records with trains. But the Secret Service took away Roosevelt's wings. No President had yet traveled by plane, and for the time being none would. In determining safety regulations, the Secret Service outranks the President.

Roosevelt would not fly again until in wartime he crossed the Atlantic partially by warship and partially by plane, because of the submarine peril, to attend the conference of Allied leaders at Tehran.

One more area should be discussed before leaving this study of Roosevelt's power center—Roosevelt's key men in Congress without whom little would have been accomplished. The President's little telephone network connecting his desk directly with these men illustrated more than anything else the blending of political ingredients upon which he hastily created the early New Deal.

To the "brain trust" might accrue much of the early credit, and some of the blame, but the Congressional votes were delivered by a handful of men unique in their time and in modern American history.

These men were the key Senators. The House of Representatives was, of course, a co-equal legislative branch, but a new President supported by a dominant majority in the House need not worry about it. With rare exceptions the House follows the President. His troubles, if any, come when legislation goes before the Senate, for two principal reasons. First, there is, as a rule, unlimited debate permitted on any issue. Second, as planned by the

Founding Fathers, Senators serve six-year terms and therefore are less tied to Party apron-strings.

Furthermore, the House, won by the Democrats in 1930, was already organized in a group that endorsed Roosevelt in the 1932 election. In the Senate, all was new; the change came only in the 1932 election, which gave the Democrats control for the first time in twelve years.

Twelve years is a long, lean time for minorities. The Democrats that survived through that period at last came into committee chairmanships and other key positions. They were tough old veterans in experience, if all were not old in years. Among them were both picturesque war horses and ambitious younger men. Each had one unchallenged vote out of only ninety-six, and a few held chairmanships that gave them dictatorial power over legislation referred to their committees. The major chairmen were hard bargainers, practical negotiators and ruthless exploiters of power. Here lay the fate of the New Deal.

Without a co-operating Senate, the New Deal would never have gone beyond vague proposals. Every major program advanced by any Administration usually requires either a law or a concurring resolution by Congress. If it involves spending money, there must be an appropriation of the money by Congress. No proclamation, whether for an emergency or not, can permit the spending of unappropriated money.

Roosevelt had known all the key Senators when he was much younger, either in the relatively small confines of Washington's official circle prior to 1920, or elsewhere as important Federal officials. He had kept closely in touch with them during his recovery from illness and his return to politics, and as they had fought for and won election and re-election and climbed the seniority ladder to positions of power. He had also the advantage of sympathetic co-operation because of his personal battle and his own personal political activities. At a Convention, for instance, he could work with them without competing in their own bailiwicks.

Five men in the Senate held a disproportionate amount of power, and it was Roosevelt's luck that they liked him and the things for which he stood. They all used their political power for his program, at least in the beginning. These five men were Carter Glass, Key Pittman, Joseph T. Robinson, Burton K. Wheeler and Robert F. Wagner.

Carter Glass, chairman of the Banking and Currency Committee, was a self-made Virginian from Lynchburg and publisher of a small but highly prosperous newspaper there.

Key Pittman, Virginia-born, parlayed a fortune on prospecting (and a little gambling) in Alaska and Nevada and by 1933 was the courtly chairman of the Foreign Relations Committee.

Joseph T. Robinson, majority leader from Arkansas, was a lawyer-politician of the old school, backed by a comfortable fortune derived from fees paid to his law firm by oil companies operating in the South.

Burton K. Wheeler was a Michigan-educated lawyer who migrated to Butte, Montana. As a crusader against the copper-mining powers he built his own machine so firmly that as a new Senator he could desert to Robert M. LaFollette's Progressive Party, campaign for the Vice-Presidency, and blithely return to his Senate seat as a Democrat.

Robert F. Wagner, who was a German immigrant raised on New York's Lower East Side, worked his way through college and law school and won a State Senate seat in the reform era. He went on to the United States Senate after serving for fourteen years on the New York State Supreme Court.

These men were senior statesmen in the Senate, and as politicians they were skilled wheelers and dealers. One of their less distinguished but eloquent colleagues Henry Fountain Ashurst of Arizona said, "The primary responsibility of a statesman is to get elected to office. His second responsibility is to stay there." These Senators knew every trick of the statesman.

When Pittman took over the seat of power formerly held by Borah, he was better known as the "silver Senator," for his success in promoting legislation which set a high price on this otherwise fairly common metal. In 1934, after his work for the foreign programs of the New Deal, he was rewarded with Administration approval of a new Silver Purchase Act.

In the meantime, Pittman had reciprocally used both his committee prestige and the votes of his mining bloc behind the measures designed to help agriculture, labor and industry.

Furthermore, Pittman used another and unorthodox lever of power. Although the Capitol had been "dry" for a generation, and Prohibition was still in effect, he could maintain without political risk a private bar in his office to which any of his colleagues were free to bring their guests.

Carter Glass, whose small stature and peppery temper won him the cloakroom nickname of "Bantam Cock," was less than enthusiastic about much of the New Deal, particularly its invasion of States rights. But in his pet field of banking and finance the Senator was a whole-souled advocate of Roosevelt's reforms. No other or greater support was needed, for Glass was the "father" of the Federal Reserve System and an advocate of tight controls over money.

Robinson as majority leader straddled many political fences without apparent conflict. Industrial leaders trusted him because of his law-practice affiliations (some critics said they paid him excessively for that support). He was interested in agriculture, for no State's farmers were harder hit by the Depression than the Arkansas cotton growers. He favored free trade because cotton prosperity or depression depended largely on the amount of exports of this overproduced crop. Furthermore, Robinson had run for the Vice-Presidency on Al Smith's 1928 ticket, and Smith was hardly an eager friend of the New Deal.

Wheeler was the maverick among the leaders, and proud of the designation. He was also a man convinced that some day he would be President. First made fairly prominent by appointment from President Wilson as District Attorney for Montana, he was elected to the Senate in 1922, where he fought for almost everything that was anathema to Robinson and Pittman. He stormed against the trusts, including the mining interests and the oil companies; he urged rigid regulation of big business. He flouted party leadership on many occasions, siding often with liberals William E. Borah of Idaho and George A. Norris of Nebraska. (Norris, a titular Republican, became a disciple of most of the New Deal.) Yet in 1933, when Wheeler became chairman of the Committee on Interstate Commerce, he served as front man for the Roosevelt Crusade.

Wagner, one of F.D.R.'s oldest political friends, saw eye-to-eye on most political matters with the President. A dignified and conservative man noted as an interpreter of the law, he was nevertheless a liberal. In time, his sphere of influence thrust him into a prominent position among authors of New Deal legislation. Yet he cherished and held the deep regard and affection of Robert A. Taft, of Ohio, one of the Senate's most conservative members.

Incidentally, Wagner lived until 1953, although he re-

tired voluntarily from the Senate in 1949 when he felt
that ill health was weakening his effectiveness. Since the
voters would gladly have kept him in his place, his retirement was unusual. In 1953, Wagner's son won the may-
oralty of New York City.

There were, of course, many others in the Senate and
in the House who helped frame the New Deal legislation, but these five were the key figures. Politics, it has
been said, makes strange bedfellows, and the political histories of these leaders surely support this view. This con-
glomerate group and its accomplishments also illustrate
that congressmen don't spend all their time in partisan
wrangling. On the floor or in the quiet councils of committee rooms and cloakrooms, they negotiate, compromise
and trade their votes, for the common good of government and, sometimes, to shoulder the "statesman's responsibility" of keeping his job.

General Hugh S. Johnson, William Bullitt, John Raskob
and F.D.R. in Warm Springs (*Wide World*)

CHAPTER 10

The Hundred Days

THE "HUNDRED DAYS" of the Roosevelt Administration lasted from the opening day of the special session of the new Congress through June 16, 1933, the finish of the first crash program.

The legislation passed in that period of absolute control by Roosevelt affected almost every detail of American life. The revolutionary steps included regulation of the stock markets, abandonment of the gold standard, guarantee of bank deposits and tight Federal controls over banking and the issuance of currency, inauguration of vast public works and provision of direct Federal aid for the needy. In none of these fields would the clock ever be turned back.

In a review of Roosevelt's career, at the time of his death, *The Times* editorial said:

The "one hundred days" of Congress rounded out a program which vested in a President for the first time in a period of peace powers which were virtually dictatorial in essence and broad in scope, which wrought changes of a fundamental and revolutionary character in the American plan of government.

Although the most urgent business was direction of domestic policy, Roosevelt also acted as his own chief director of foreign affairs in disarmament, opposition to the dictatorships and efforts to cement what remained of the alliance of Western democracies.

After completion of the emergency measures concerning banking, currency and gold, the New Deal appeared to relax momentarily. The quiet was deceptive, however. This was a period of preparation for new laws and programs, and of negotiations with congressional leaders to assure ultimate passage of the bills.

Then, as a surprise to most observers, there came a side bit of legislation not on the emergency agenda, the legalization of 3.2 beer—based on the assumption that such a small alcoholic percentage was nonintoxicating. It was a stopgap in the repeal of Prohibition. Congress had already passed the repeal amendment, but ratification by the States would take a long time.

What this measure did in effect was to get the breweries back into legal business, reopen a legitimate market for vast quantities of grain and create new tax receipts.

March passed without enactment of any major national legislation, but it was marked by intensive committee hearings and floor debates on new programs in both Houses of Congress.

In April, Roosevelt used his emergency powers to establish a combined reforestation and employment program, the Civilian Conservation Corps. On the eighth day of that month, the first twenty-five thousand city youths volunteering in the program reported to the Army posts nearest them for enrollment in the corps.

Although carefully separated from the soldiers, they

slept in spare barracks, ate in military mess halls, and marched in groups to and from the woods where they worked. The only penalty for disobedience was dismissal. Otherwise they received one dollar a day and their keep, plus a guarantee of continued relief payments to their parents or families.

On this same April day, a distinguished British author stopped in New York to give the country some gratuitous but unwelcome advice. George Bernard Shaw paused in a world tour to give a highly profitable lecture in the Metropolitan Opera House. The substance of his speech was that the United States should "scrap the Constitution," cancel all war debts and nationalize the banks. He angered most Americans (which he delighted to do) and embarrassed the national government, which feared that critics might think the old Fabian Socialist had some advance dope.

April, too, passed rather uneventfully in Washington, but questions began to arise as to what end the New Deal was taking the country. Roosevelt already had been on the radio to discuss the question, but he and his inner circle thought it time to enlighten the public again. Another fireside chat was set for May 7, this one to be directed mainly to the country's businessmen. In it, Roosevelt made no commitments but promised "a partnership between business and government in national planning." He predicted a good, strong future for the dollar.

On May 12, the Congress passed a law providing the first $500,000,000 for direct relief of the unemployed. The law cleverly avoided "appropriating" this money from the hard-pressed Treasury. Instead, it "directed" the Reconstruction Finance Corporation, a government lending agency for making business loans, to provide the money. Half would go to the States as direct grants-in-aid for their relief programs; the other half would be distributed on the basis of each State putting up three dollars for each additional dollar given to it. No repayment ever was to be made by the States.

A week later, Harry L. Hopkins appeared on the Washington scene. He was unknown to most people except as a professional welfare worker from New York City; he had held neither a public office nor any position with important public responsibilities. Hopkins was named Federal Relief Administrator, nevertheless, and was given temporary offices in an empty office building leased by the government. Direct relief was under way, with the injunction from Roosevelt: "Get this money out fast!"

Both the money provided and the scope of Hopkins' authority were deliberately made to appear deceptively small. The New Deal leaders would have to work hard to condition the public to think in terms of the relief they anticipated. But even $500,000,000 was a frightening sum in 1933.

At that time the entire Federal Government was running on an overall budget of about $4,000,000,000 a year. The entire annual budget in 1933 would, in 1965, support the government for no longer than two weeks.

A week after the relief bill, the Congress passed another law, not particularly controversial at the time, but more revolutionary in its long-run results than most other legislation passed in the "hundred days." This bill authorized the establishment of the Tennessee Valley Authority and put the $165,000,000 water-power project designed for World War I munitions manufacture to work producing nitrates for cheap fertilizer.

Muscle Shoals was an old project sponsored by a group of agriculturists led by Senator George A. Norris, the radical Republican from Nebraska. Its sponsors also envisioned enlargement of the power facilities on the Tennessee River at Muscle Shoals, Alabama so that the surplus might be sold cheaply to help electrify farming in the depressed regions of the river valley. The fear that government might compete with private enterprise had kept the bill dormant. The sponsors had answered this objection with the argument that anything that TVA might do would be in a field too large, too expensive, and too lacking in profit to warrant private development.

Now, however, the door had been opened. Arthur E. Morgan was named as Chairman of TVA, and David E. Lilienthal was appointed as a member of the Authority. These appointments and that of Hopkins all were dated May 19.

Before May ended, the President also received and signed two other major laws, one canceling the gold clause in all contracts (mentioned earlier) and the other authorizing broad regulation of all securities exchanges. The gold-clause act completely eliminated claims for gold in payment of anything; henceforth the dollar was a dollar whenever and wherever the United States Government said that it was. The Securities Exchange Act also was permanent legislation, wiping out peculiar tax advantages for wealthy traders. It was endorsed by practitioners of the art of finance like Joseph P. Kennedy, Bernard M. Baruch, and James V. Forrestal.

Congress ended its historic session at 1:38 A.M. on June 16 with passage of two final measures, one the National Industrial Recovery Act and the other the Glass-Steagall Banking Bill. The NIRA established the National Recovery Administration (NRA), the capstone of New Deal changes. The Banking Bill clearly stated in law, as distinguished from Presidential emergency action, the authority of the Federal Government over all banking.

Between signing these new laws and departing in the evening for his first vacation since the Inaugural, the President named as NRA Administrator General Hugh

S. Johnson, colorful, retired cavalry officer and industrial executive.

On the same hectic day, Roosevelt allocated $400,000,-000 of public funds for the construction of State roads, and he set aside the hypothetical sum of $238,000,000 for the start of construction of thirty-two new warships. The appropriation for State roads, in contrast to "post roads" already financed by the Federal Government, established a new precedent in spending. It also created employment and improved the highways of the country. The public was told that the naval construction program—the largest single lump sum allocated until that time—was instituted to create work in the coastal cities where shipyards were most idle.

During the "hundred days," Roosevelt also had been drafting other important personnel to staff the New Deal. For these additional offices he drew largely on a few well-known old hands in government and a number of prominent conservatives. His political sense seemed to impel him to maintain a defendable balance between the "activists" he was bringing into his revolutionary program and the conservatives who would give evidence of traditionalism. Few of these appointees, however, were previously identified as politicians; none was particularly prominent in leadership of the Democratic Party.

The leaders of the Democratic machines in such cities as New York, Boston and Chicago had assumed they held a mortgage on patronage under the new Administration; they were mistaken. Some of their hurt feelings were soothed, however, by the generous allocation of relief funds to their cities. Few among these newly appointed men made "headlines" at the time, but modern readers will remember several of them for their subsequent prominence.

First alphabetically was the tall, aristocratic corporate lawyer, Dean G. Acheson, then forty years old. Son of a former Episcopal bishop of Connecticut, honor graduate of Harvard Law School and former law clerk to Justice Brandeis, Acheson in 1933 was a partner in a high-ranking law firm specializing in corporate and international practice. He became Under Secretary of the Treasury and right hand to Secretary Woodin.

J. C. Biggs was made Solicitor General in the Department of Justice, under Attorney General Cummings, to prepare the defenses for eventual court trials challenging many of the New Deal laws.

Robert W. Bingham, wealthy publisher of the *Louisville Courier-Journal,* famous nationally but inexperienced in foreign affairs, was named Ambassador to the Court of St. James's, a post that then could be occupied only by a man of great wealth. Eugene R. Black, born in Atlanta, Georgia, and already a noted banking expert, became a Governor of the Federal Reserve Board. Claude G. Bowers, the noted historian and a lay leader in the Catholic Church, was made Ambassador to Spain.

In the State Department, where Moley already was an Assistant Secretary, W. J. Carr, a career man, was named to the same relative position; and W. C. Bullitt, wealthy and scholarly Philadelphian, was designated a "special assistant." Bullitt was assigned specifically to the study of Soviet Russia in preparation for becoming the first Ambassador to Soviet Russia.

Oscar L. Chapman, energetic young lawyer from the Northwest, who had founded the Young Democrats of America as a political arm of Roosevelt's presidential campaign, joined Secretary Ickes as Assistant Secretary of the Interior.

John F. Cudahy, American businessman without the least tinge of communist leanings, was named Ambassador to Poland, then in a difficult position with Russia.

Josephus Daniels, newspaper publisher in Raleigh, North Carolina, and Roosevelt's Navy chief in World War I, was made Ambassador to Mexico in a period when there was controversy over American claims against that government. His task was to maintain friendship despite the disputes and arguments, in line with the "good neighbor policy."

Joseph B. Eastman moved into Washington to start a long career in regulation of transportation as railroad co-ordinator, under plans to assist the railroads to regain their depression-thwarted prosperity and to modernize their facilities.

Joseph C. Grew, courtly and mature career diplomat, was sent to Tokyo as Ambassador to Japan, to report upon and work toward checking Asian conquests by the militarists who had seized power. Ambassador Grew was helpless to achieve his mission, but the State Department files were enriched by his many detailed, prescient reports. Each began with a greeting to the Secretary of State and continued: "I have the honor to transmit these jottings from my diary."

Henry Morgenthau, Jr., New York financier and a Dutchess County neighbor of Roosevelt, appeared in Washington as Chairman of the Federal Farm Board. His task was to administer the new farm assistance program. The tall, humorless official was the son of a distinguished American Jewish diplomat. The new administrator could not guess that before a year had passed he would become Secretary of the Treasury.

Not announced in the "hundred days," but already decided, was another appointment important to the heart of the New Deal revolution. Ickes was named Emergency Administrator of Public Works, an additional responsibility to his Cabinet position.

While building the New Deal foundations in these early days, Roosevelt found an amazing amount of time to devote to foreign policy—or so it seemed. Although he was greatly concerned about the domestic situation, he was worried, almost fearful, about events abroad. He saw that world of 1933 as one in which the United States had few friends; those it had were distrustful of the isolationist sentiment which marked most American discussion of foreign affairs.

In the years since World War I, the League of Nations had become a dead issue; it was not acceptable to Americans. An adjunct to the League but separate from it was the World Court, designed to resolve great issues between nations. Even it was anathema to the controlling bloc in the Senate headed by William Edgar Borah.

At every new Congress under Presidents Harding, Coolidge and Hoover, the Chief Executives had requested the Senate to approve articles of adherence to the Court. Every attempt was defeated.

One dramatic evidence of Roosevelt's deep fear of developments in Germany was a remark made "completely off the record" to a small group of reporters; and years later the statement was verified by events. It is important also in understanding his efforts toward friendship with Russia.

Roosevelt had been informed that German steel works were turning out highly specialized large tubings described as housings for propeller shafts of large ships. But these tubings were appearing in such large quantities that no fleets could ever make use of them; the "blanks" were identical with the castings from which barrels for heavy cannons could be forged. The implications were obvious.

Yet these fears could not be discussed openly. The word for such public statements then was "warmongering."

This meant that Roosevelt was confined in foreign relations to official functions, state visits and similar meetings. A trip abroad would have been politically unthinkable at this time.

In his second month in office, April of 1933, Roosevelt received the first foreign visitors from three major countries, Britain, France and Canada.

Ramsay MacDonald, of Britain, headed a tenuous coalition government in his Parliament, and Edouard Herriot was temporarily on top in the French Republic's game of musical chairs. R. B. Bennett, Prime Minister of the sparsely populated country to the north, came to Washington from Canada, which was a firm friend and both the largest seller to, and customer of, the United States.

In comparison with the pilgrimages of 1945 through 1965, foreign rulers were hardly flocking to Washington, but among larger countries these three were about the only friends we had.

It is interesting to twirl a globe of the world and recapture the picture of the relative importance of countries in the 1930s. During that period the foundations of the United States world position thirty years later were being laid.

In that twirling glance, obliterate all of Africa as a world force except the Union of South Africa, and remember that South Africa has never been much of a power. Look at South America as a continent of great pride, generally friendly to the United States but with only a few spots of common interest with North America.

Russia in the '30s was a gigantic cauldron of revolution, but a threat more as an exporter of revolution than as a military or economic force. India and China were the subjects of romantic stories but were outside the common range of interest or of knowledge. Japan was seen in the

United States principally as an exporter of cut-rate manufactured goods then flooding the American market.

What was left of importance to the United States? Some of Europe and Canada. Yet in Europe, Germany and Italy had become more and more hostile. There were friends among the smaller countries, but they could only drift with the tide. This left Great Britain and France—Britain not very stable and France not stable at all.

Economically Canada, our relatively small neighbor, was more important than either Britain or France. These three—Britain, France and Canada—were the only major allies we had in the struggle for the economic recovery of the world.

The political leaders of this pitifully small group of "powers" descended on Washington—aging men, all of whom headed dying regimes. Their accompanying staffs exchanged notes with State Department officials while the chiefs met with the President.

For Roosevelt, the week of April 22 was a series of educational conferences on foreign affairs much like a college cram session, broken each evening by the ludicrous necessity of formal dinners.

In that week the White House kitchens prepared and served three distinct but similar state dinners for the visiting chiefs of state. In turn, each visitor entertained the President at his embassy or legation (Canada did not yet have embassy status). On the seventh night Roosevelt held an informal stag dinner for Herriot and Bennett. He also devoted one afternoon to a private talk with MacDonald during a chilly cruise down the Potomac aboard *Sequoia*.

There was more significance than would be understood for years in this hectic week of token conferences. Roosevelt attempted, with an appearance of confidence which masked his real confusion and ignorance, to catch up hurriedly with the hopeful and questioning views which other countries held of his election and new recovery policies.

Others also were watching with hope and alarm the gestures of Washington in this New Deal—the people in small European states and their immigrant minorities in the United States.

Among these groups were the Polish people. There was a White House dinner of March 21, a month before the onslaught of major visitors, given in honor of Ignace J. Paderewski. In the eyes of most Americans the dinner honored the man who probably was the world's greatest living pianist. To many educated Europeans, and particularly to Poles, it seemed the White House was reaffirming its regard for the former Polish Prime Minister in a period when Poland was hovering between the pincers of Nazism on the west and communism on the east.

The absence of others who might have visited Washington had special significance. At this time Germany and Italy maintained lavish embassies in Washington and Japan had just completed one of the capital's most beautiful structures for its new embassy.

Representatives of none of these countries visited the new President. For all of Roosevelt's political astuteness, he had never officially visited any foreign country nor had an opportunity to talk with officials of other governments. Neither had Secretary Hull, whose political background as a Representative and Senator from Tennessee made it almost political suicide to be "friendly with foreigners."

It became essential, therefore, for Roosevelt to establish contact with America's friends and to urge them to take steps that would restore American confidence in them.

Ironically the French Embassy spoiled much that might otherwise have been accomplished. When Roosevelt was elected, the French Foreign Office "experts" planned a coup in the manner of old-style diplomacy. In the upper ranks of the career foreign service was Andre de Laboulaye, who had served as a secretary at the French Embassy in Washington when Roosevelt was Assistant Secretary of the Navy. The de Laboulayes and the Roosevelts had become friends.

Because of the friendship the former secretary was appointed Ambassador to the United States, and his arrival was carefully planned for March 10, right after the flurry of the Inaugural.

The de Laboulayes arrived on schedule, and the Roosevelts were delighted. The State Department went about arranging for the Ambassador's first official call on the President and presentation of his credentials.

However, Mrs. Roosevelt decided it would be a special sign of friendship to go immediately and greet Madame de Laboulaye, and renew their personal friendship. On the morning of March 11 she got into her car and drove to the French Embassy. This visit was completely unofficial.

In the intervening years, the French Ambassador's lady had become stuffed with protocol, but not with diplomatic discretion. By mid-afternoon she was telling friends, including the group of newspaper "society writers" who are indigenous to the Washington scene, that she was "amazed" that Mrs. Roosevelt came unannounced to the Embassy before her husband had been received formally at the White House!

So ended the carefully planned diplomatic coup. While Americans cheered Mrs. Roosevelt for her human gesture, and Sir Ronald Lindsay at the British Embassy chuckled over the report, the Madame de Laboulaye's snobbish remark lashed back on the French. De Laboulaye was duly received and took his formal place in the diplomatic corps, but he obviously never enjoyed a single confidential conversation with the President, or even believed what he could easily read in the newspapers. Eventually the Ambassador had to be recalled because of misinformed reports to his government that Roosevelt certainly would join the appeasers of Hitler.

The "hundred days" passed, Congress adjourned and the New Deal was underway. Roosevelt could relax. He sent some new instructions to Norman Davis, who continued to represent the United States at the Geneva Disarmament Conference and was about to return home and report. He cabled Hull, concerning the opening on June 16 of the British-called World Economic Conference in London.

In the evening he boarded a special train to Boston for his first vacation since the Inaugural, a boating excursion off the coast of New England, followed by a covey of reporters assigned to follow him to sea.

So much had happened in the past three months—so many unprecedented events had taken place. Unique, too, was the trip about to begin.

F.D.R. on *Amberjack II* (*Wide World*)

CHAPTER 11

F.D.R., Yachtsman

ONCE A RATHER PREVALENT DISTRUST of yachtsmen was noticeable in the American electorate. Men who made their living by going to sea were generally respected. But if they went to sea for fun, the public felt that they were rich or idle or both. Neither quality was desirable in a country whose folklore was built on poverty and the common man.

Of course, right up to the Depression and through it, millions of Americans were prosperous and urbane, and lots of them wanted yachts. But a yachtsman was a different type of sportsman from a rabbit- or duck-hunter. Politically speaking, the Victorian and Edwardian era had developed a feeling even among prosperous Americans that yachting (except small-boat fishing excursions) was a stiffly formal hobby of millionaires out of touch with the people. What was worse, it was also the sport of Englishmen.

This attitude would certainly cause amusement today among the six million or so owners of power and sailing craft. In the '30s, however, it was still a popular custom for vaudeville comedians to retell J. P. Morgan's reputed remark, "If you wonder how much it will cost to operate a yacht, you can't afford one."

And here was Roosevelt, to the dismay of his political managers—in addition to his other "handicaps" of family and wealth—an ardent yachtsman. He never owned one of the "you-can't-afford-one" size, but he consorted with people who did—some of them very respectable people indeed, but not in the public eye. Even President Hoover, who was richer than most yacht owners of the period and who loved to go deep-sea fishing, indulged his hobby without fanfare. Hoover had also placed in dry dock the old *Mayflower,* which from the time of the Spanish-American War had been the top-heavy, unseaworthy and extravagant Presidential yacht.

Only "Teddy" Roosevelt had ever used *Mayflower* much, and then only for week-end cruises on the Potomac. He did give it a place in history when, in quest for absolute negotiating privacy, *Mayflower* was the meeting place for negotiators who wrote the terms for ending the Russo-Japanese War.

During Roosevelt's campaign for the Presidency his backers obviously never mentioned his yachting background or skill, as a reason for electing him to the Presidency. Only after his victory did he draw attention to his association with the sport by going for a cruise in January on *Nourmahal* to the Bahamas.

Nevertheless, we were to learn that he was at heart a real salt and an offshore or deep-water sailor, in contrast to an inland or shallow-water sailor. His seafaring Delano ancestors seemed to have left him another legacy.

Our little group of reporters had to absorb all this suddenly in a few hours on a foggy June morning at Marion, Massachusetts. The extent of the sea voyage came as a shock. But the manner in which Roosevelt proved himself a rugged sailor added only one more stroke to a portrait of virility. I believed then, and still believe, that this activity was as deliberately designed for political reasons as it was for recreation.

Certainly there were more comfortable ways for a President to indulge his love of the water than to spend most of three weeks, rain or shine, halted only by fog, in the open cockpit of a schooner riding out the Atlantic swells.

The main set piece of this act was the forty-five-foot schooner *Amberjack II*. But the four news correspondents observed from the slightly smaller but relatively luxurious power craft, the auxiliary ketch *Mary Alice*. Neither I nor the other three had a yacht in our backgrounds, but we put to sea in line of duty. At first hand each experienced the rain, fog, and choppy ocean, rode the swells and tides, and made the night passage into Gloucester, Massachusetts, past "the Reef of Norman's Woe." Each of us, after some initial queasiness, had the most wonderful experiences supported by expense accounts.

By the time Roosevelt had been in office for three months, it was known that he loved the water, but most people had only vague impressions of his tastes. Most people thought he liked sailing in luxurious comfort, since they first viewed him aboard *Nourmahal,* a vessel some three hundred feet long and reputedly the largest yacht at the time—a veritable small ocean liner. She was equipped for, and perfectly able to carry out, voyages to the South Seas in quest of the marine studies that were Astor's hobby.

Once inaugurated, Roosevelt was tied to his White House routine for more than three months, but the first warm days in April found him eagerly going out for day or week-end excursions on a government boat, the old *Sequoia*. In private hands she would have been a very decent yacht, but in government service she was termed by the politically safer designation of houseboat.

Sequoia was owned originally by the Commerce Department for use of the Bureau of Coastal and Geodetic Survey. It served Roosevelt for many years. Later, after World War II, when President Truman got the former Chrysler yacht, *Sequoia* became more or less an entertainment craft for the Cabinet.

By April 23, 1933, *Sequoia* became part of the news of the time, when President Roosevelt took aboard her as his guest, for a cruise on the Potomac and Chesapeake Bay, Prime Minister Ramsay MacDonald, of Great Britain.

It soon became apparent that Roosevelt was making *Sequoia* his favorite retreat from the telephones and daily routine of his office. He used it for private conferences, for speech-writing and for relaxation, and he continued to used it right up to the frosty October weather, when chilly air and fall winds made life out of doors on the deck uncomfortable. But this was still yachting, despite the "houseboat" designation, on a small ship with plenty of service, staterooms with private baths, a well-equipped galley and steam heat.

Thus, when the White House announced around the first of June that soon after Roosevelt had tidied up urgent matters he would go for a cruise in New England waters, most interested persons pictured this as another yachting trip or perhaps a voyage on a warship. The subsequent announcement that Roosevelt had chartered through his son James the schooner *Amberjack II* did nothing to dispel the illusion. And those reporters assigned to go with him were cheered by the added confidential report that James also was arranging—at the newspapers' expense—for a boat for the escorting press.

The realities of the new assignment, shattering the reporters' dreams of luxury, dawned starkly upon the press party on the morning of June 16. After a drive from Boston where the President left his private train, they arrived in bleak weather at the seaside village of Marion, Massachusetts.

The President went to *Amberjack,* waiting in a remote mooring chosen for security reasons, and the reporters went as directed to a rendezvous with the press boat. At a slight distance, its length of fifty-five feet, white and clean, looked elegant.

The eight newsmen boarded this boat only to find that it had been assigned to sleep at most eight passengers without baggage on a one-night cruise, with one crew member. But this cruise required a crew of three. Moreover, the crew must have decided that with a charter of landlubbers they could make up for a long hungry spell. They had taken the best quarters. The boat, which will remain nameless, was much less than clean. In any event, it was too small. New arrangements needed to be made quickly. But traveling correspondents are used to fast changes of plans.

In the party were four press association reporters and four staff correspondents for individual newspapers. The press association men had to start, and start quickly, to be on hand when *Amberjack* hoisted her sails and set out that forenoon. They took over that first boat.

The four "specials," to whom I belonged, had some hours to spare because we all wrote for morning newspapers; the filing of dispatches could wait until afternoon. So back to the dock went the luggage, typewriters and baggage of the four of us. The other boat hoisted anchor and started to its rendezvous. At a considerable distance we could still hear the arguments about living arrangements between the crew and the news agency men.

Then our group suddenly realized what it had done. We were on an assignment; but we had no boat, no directions, and really no idea where we were. Bill Murphy, of the *New York World,* after making a few unsubtle comments on James' arrangements, said, "How the hell do you charter a boat up here?"

Ernest K. Lindley, the senior companion and writer for the *New York Herald Tribune,* looked around at the empty dock and said, "Maybe we better go uptown, if there is an 'uptown.' "

John Herrick, of the *Chicago Tribune* and therefore the worst landlubber of all, reminded us that no reporter is ever defeated on an assignment. "Let's look in a telephone book." It was agreed that this was a practical suggestion, if a telephone directory could be found.

At this moment, a smart-looking Navy gig from a destroyer that was to be part of the President's escort showed up to check on the progress of the correspondents. The Navy had been cautioned not to lose any newsmen— bad publicity. It is an old political rule that politicians may snub newspapermen, sometimes try to fool them, and sometimes try to manipulate their stories; but they never abandon them or do anything that might make the press really angry.

The rating in charge of the gig had heard from the first press boat that the special correspondents had not started, and he had come to offer help. He agreed that the plan to find a telephone book for the search had merit, but he was dubious. However, his orders required him to return quickly to his mother ship; the best he could promise was to return or send another dispatch boat after a few hours.

Murphy and Lindley, being senior to Herrick and me, volunteered to remain with the little mountain of luggage and wait for a report. Thereupon they sat down to read the morning newspapers. Herrick and I started on foot toward what looked like the center of the town. We finally found a telephone book in a booth in a filling station.

In the classified section, under Yacht Brokers, was one name with a Marion address. It was that of Charles Furnans. That was the beginning of a streak of luck that would make any Las Vegas habitué envious.

Furnans was at home. At first he thought we were joking about wanting a charter yacht right then. The Secret Service had ordered us not to mention the President's cruise until he was at sea, and the story we created may have been flimsy. Eventually Furnans believed one tale sufficiently to invite us to his nearby house to talk about it. He must have been intrigued, because when we arrived he had hot coffee waiting.

We had to tell him the truth then, but found he already knew that F.D.R. was involved. Because of generous expense advances, we could show him enough money to pay substantially in advance. His doubts resolved, Furnans got right to the point. He had a boat of his own, *Mary Alice,* which in those days was an extravagant luxury. She had never been chartered but we could hire her. He thought that in an hour or so he could round up a skipper and a necessary "crew" to keep the boat clean, help with docking lines and otherwise be useful.

Because of the unemployment situation around coastal villages, Furnans was able to solve the personnel problem quickly. While he was telephoning we had a fast breakfast. Then he drove us to a cove where his boat was in the water. He took along the carburetor, which he had kept in clean storage, and installed it in *Mary Alice* himself.

Never was there a more helpful man. We never saw

Furnans again, since we discharged *Mary Alice* at East-port, Maine; but each of us thanked him and mentioned his name and charter service in our dispatches. In that summer *Mary Alice* became as much publicized as *Amberjack II,* if not as important.

Herrick and I went directly to the boat without detour-ing to consult our colleagues. They were comfortably set-tled to wait for us, even though it was raining by now. We couldn't waste time.

Mary Alice was not an ordinary boat. She had been built by a man who insisted on comfort with his sport, and in a time when cost was relatively unimportant. Her wide, high hull was thirty-eight feet long. Deep-sea fish-ing was her principal function; her appearance could not compare with the sleek looks of the week-end pleasure boats. She had a bow pulpit for harpooning sailfish and tuna, but no nonsense like modern flying-bridges or multi-hundred horsepower engines for excessive speed.

Mary Alice's accommodations consisted of a roomy cockpit, with canvas side curtains for protection in choppy weather; a generous main cabin that could sleep four persons in folding bunks, or that could be used as a fairly large sitting room; a tiny forward cabin for two others; and a private cabin for the captain, an unusual feature. But the items which contributed most to our comfort in the squally weeks ahead were the sails that made the boat an auxiliary ketch.

Mary Alice was powered by an engine that delivered an easy ten miles per hour, which would be useful for going ashore, filing dispatches and returning to the con-voy. But two stubby masts—we learned to call them "main" and "mizzen"—held sails that gave very little speed even in a brisk wind. However, when a breeze filled them the boat seemed to stiffen in the water and seldom rolled at all.

In four hours, Furnans and the ship's company sailed to the dock to pick up our two waiting companions. Having no idea of what had been done in so short a time they were a little curt in their first greetings and complained of being wet and hungry. Herrick and I thought there was perhaps a touch of envy in their reactions: since we were first on board we had taken over the little private cabin, leaving for them the folding bunks in the larger common cabin. But by the time the Navy boat came back to fetch us, all was serene.

It took a little longer to overcome the envy of the press association colleagues, and we had the impression that the President never quite felt the same about his own boat after seeing *Mary Alice*. *Amberjack* was a true sportsman's yacht and technically a safer one, since its cooking stove was fired with coal instead of bottled gas. But the stove made extra dirt, and the engine of *Amberjack* was much less powerful than *Mary Alice's* so that without wind in its sails the yacht was very slow. There were no means of protecting the cockpit with canvas when it rained. When rain fell on the Presidential yacht, it fell equally on the skipper at the wheel.

Mary Alice also had, because of the good advice and foresight of Furnans, a small luxury that came under the fading but still legal cloud of Prohibition. Furnans had advised that such "ship's stores" would be highly desirable. A case of reliable Bourbon whisky somehow materialized as he patiently guided us through the maze of shopping for provisions while *Mary Alice* was being put into active commission.

In mid-afternoon, guided by the Navy gig, *Mary Alice* joined the convoy and took her place near the other press boat, perhaps a quarter mile from *Amberjack*. This distance protected the President's privacy but enabled the reporters to see through field glasses the President at the wheel, seated in the open cockpit, slicker and sou'wester protecting him from spray, and even his cigarette holder uptilted at a jaunty angle.

When we anchored that night in Edgartown for the first stop on the cruise, we sent off our dispatches under the dateline, "At Sea with President Roosevelt" (a dateline that gave rise to a number of interpretations).

Since Roosevelt was the first President with a taste for such cruising, the arrangements for this excursion are of some interest. As much detail was involved, and almost as many humorous incidents, as any chapter in the personal histories of the Presidents. The reasons for the detail, however, should not be considered lightly; those officials responsible for the arrangements were simply scared to death.

Their fear was exclusively for the President's safety. It was shared by the Secret Service, which held his life as its responsibility; by the Coast Guard, in whose jurisdictional waters he was and which, like the Secret Service, was another branch of the Treasury; and by the Navy, which had to provide the "outer escort" and communications services for its Commander-in-Chief.

These groups all had had a share in protecting other Presidents on the water. But the plans always had involved trips at sea in much larger vessels, or the lighter task of overseeing fishing excursions in protected waters.

Roosevelt, however, was at sea in a relatively small yacht—one small enough to be swamped in a storm while he rode the open waters of the Atlantic Ocean.

Only Roosevelt's amateur crew manned *Amberjack,* and in 1933 there were no ship-to-shore telephones or, for that matter, small wireless telegraph sets with which to call for emergency help if fog or wind separated *Amberjack* from her escort. Under such circumstances a boat can be very much alone.

There were other fears, too, in the mind of Colonel Starling, chief of the Secret Service, such as danger from kidnappers or the gangsters whose bootleg hijacking operations marked all of this coastline.

The escorts simply had to do the best they could in the face of Roosevelt's determination to cruise in *Amberjack* just like any other yachtsmen.

Riding near to the President but under strict orders from him not to come so close as to spoil his feeling of privacy was a patrol boat containing a Secret Service detail. The boat coasted along during the daytime, its speed throttled down to the sailing pace of *Amberjack*. At anchorages this boat cruised in a circle around the schooner. Actually, there were several of these boats, since the men had to be relieved of their watch at intervals.

The "mother ship" for these boats was an ocean-going Coast Guard cutter, aboard which lived Secretary McIntyre with a small White House staff and the Secret Service personnel. Augmenting the cutter's work were two Navy destroyers. Farther at sea was the cruiser *Indianapolis*. As far as practicable, Navy seaplanes patrolled the air on the lookout for unexpected trouble, and other airplanes flew twice daily between the cutter and Washington with dispatch bags and occasional official visitors.

In the meantime, on shore, other Secret Service details moved from point to point by automobiles, to examine and plot possible anchorages and arrange for stopping places in the event of bad weather or emergencies. Detailed plans were made for hasty rescue of the President in the event of illness or threats to his life. A Navy officer later confided that the destroyers had rigged special slings and gear to hoist the President off *Amberjack* if such hasty action became necessary. (What they would have given for a modern helicopter!)

Fortunately the actual cruise afforded less drama than had been prepared for. In fact, with the exception of two newsworthy political episodes, the cruise was so uneventful that we had to write about how the President handled his boat, the weather, and anything else that we could develop into a news story. One day we even kept count of the gulls that hovered over *Amberjack*.

This kind of news writing brought new hazards for the reporters, who would listen attentively to the jargon of the sea in which *Mary Alice's* captain described what *Amberjack* was doing and then try to condense and translate this into news stories.

That hazard was not a light one, as one pitfall that trapped me will illustrate. On one change of course, Roosevelt ordered a shift in sails. I thought that he had "reefed the jib," and I used the phrase in a story. *The Times'* copy reader—doubtless another landlubber since our dispatches were considered "political news" and not sports stories—did not edit this phrase from the story.

More than four hundred gleeful fault-finders among the denizens of Long Island Sound wrote to *The Times* alone to point out that *anyone would know* you never reef a jib; you either take it in or put it out. A reporter may forget an historic date, but never a mistake that draws that many corrections.

As the cruise became more routine we got to know another side of Roosevelt, and he perhaps got a new impression of newspaper reporters. From June 16 to June 29, the flotilla anchored at points from Cape Cod all the way to Campobello, opposite Eastport; we docked in historic places like Nantucket, Gloucester, Portland, as well as many little-known coves. We reporters slept and lived aboard our craft, but had to go ashore sometimes to file dispatches. Once, when the normal thirty-foot tide was at lowest ebb, all of us climbed a slime-coated ladder to a pier to find the Western Union office. Twice, there was an opportunity to go ashore and have real baths in hotels. But it was never safe to go very far away.

People came and went aboard *Amberjack*. Roosevelt's various sons and friends were invited to take their honored turns as crew members alongside Paul R. Rust, Jr., owner of the boat. Mrs. Roosevelt paid a call on her husband at Southeast Harbor, Maine. Two officials, Moley and Norman H. Davis, were flown to rendezvous with the President.

All the reporters had a rather leisurely time—only one story a day to dispatch; no speeches or parades or "whistle stops." The press association reporters were busier, filing at least two stories daily, one for the afternoon and one for the morning papers.

On the other press boat were four men who had been with Roosevelt since his election: Francis Stephenson, of the Associated Press; Frederick A. Storm, of United Press; George A. Durno, of International News Service, and Edward A. Roddan, of Universal News Service.

Both etiquette and Roosevelt's physical handicap prevented him from visiting our boats, but occasionally he invited us aboard his own. We went in separate contingents, since *Amberjack* did not have enough cockpit or cabin room to handle eight guests. We soon established a good rapport on the basis of a mutual understanding that never was reported at the time. Some things are strictly between friends.

On one of our first visits to *Amberjack,* the President inquired, at first in solicitous detail, as to how we were faring. He wished us to be comfortable, and was genuinely concerned. But when we responded to his questions —as to our eating, sleeping and comfort—his expression changed. We lived better than he did.

He asked us what we had established as routine aboard
Mary Alice where, in his eyes, to be a passenger must be
a monotonous life. We replied that we wrote, ate, slept
and caught up on our reading, and then relaxed with
cocktails after we had anchored for the night and sent
off our dispatches.

The following conversation is reported accurately in
substance if not in detail.

The President: "Drinking? Have you got liquor on
board?"

Reporter: "We have a few medicinal supplies, Mr.
President."

The President: "Well, that's all right—especially since
you're not accustomed to the cold and wet. You have
enough?"

Reporter: "We are husbanding it carefully, sir. You're
very thoughtful. How about yourself?"

The President (speaking firmly): "Of course, we've no
liquor. For the time being this boat is a commissioned
Navy craft. The Navy is dry."

Reporter: "We had thought . . . it's too bad you can't
join us, sir."

The President (impatiently): "But we have ice and
glasses and water, and if someone would occasionally
bring along . . ."

Reporter (reaching for a bottle rolled in his rain coat):
"Mr. President, we'd be honored."

The President (pointing): "You'll find the ice chest in
the galley forward. And the glasses are on a shelf just
above it."

Before Roosevelt sailed off in *Amberjack,* he had told
some of his intimates that he wished to see how well things
in Washington would run in his absence.

The initial legislation of the New Deal had been

passed, major projects had been outlined, and most of the key posts had been filled with appointees. Some appointments were still under his consideration while he was away, but we began to see a pattern for his future program.

The President saved two decisions dealing with foreign crises for conferences on his vacation: one concerning the stalemate in disarmament talks and the other concerning the clamor of Europe for American leadership in reversing the world-wide depression. These talks at sea were dramatic enough to make headlines, but that was about all. One so angered Hull that he almost resigned, and the other added to the worry of America's friends abroad.

The appointment of Hull as Secretary of State had been intended as a signal to all the world that in economic affairs, as well as political relations, the United States firmly intended to be a "good neighbor." Hull played up U.S. concern for Latin America in every possible way. And he began the delicate and hazardous negotiations leading to later diplomatic recognition of Soviet Russia, thus opening a door for conversation at least.

The incident which almost precipitated Hull's resignation was a meeting between Moley and Roosevelt. Moley was carried by train, seaplane and boat for private conferences aboard *Amberjack* on June 20. Newspaper correspondents did not see him. The only announcement was that he was going to London as "personal representative" of the President. Nothing could have infuriated Hull more. Who was making policy, he asked; who was the boss?

The second seaboard conference concerned disarmament. Keeping Norman H. Davis as chief of the American mission to the Disarmament Conference in Geneva emphasized the Roosevelt Administration's good intentions to continue the work begun two years earlier under

Hoover. In May, Roosevelt had sent an urgent plea for results to the fifty-four participating nations in Geneva.

The Davis visit was conducted in an entirely different manner from the secret meeting with Moley. On the assumption that he had arrived earlier than expected, he was brought by boat to *Mary Alice* for an informal background chat with the "specials" on the many problems besetting the Geneva conference. For an hour he lounged in the cabin, while fog swirled around our anchored boat (the flotilla was held immobile at Roque Island). He talked entertainingly and illuminatingly.

It was evident that no great power really meant to disarm, particularly not Germany, Japan nor Russia. But his message was that we must get the best deal we could and—having already destroyed most of our power under earlier disarmament agreements—build up to the maximum under the hoped-for new agreements.

This conversation took place on June 26, 1933. Davis went on to confer with Roosevelt. No communiqué was issued concerning their conference.

Within months, however, even more funds were found within the scope of the great new Public Works Program to hurry along the building of "treaty warships" as a means of restoring jobs in the country's shipyards, and to stimulate employment in the ranks of the subcontractors. This marked the beginning of the Navy build-up, which provided the United States with the few modern ships it had when it became involved in World War II. The plans for the build-up came in part from that meeting with Norman Davis.

In that interview on *Mary Alice,* Davis related an incident which demonstrated how much the United States actually had disarmed. Some event in Cuba, he said, called for the sending of a cruiser on a courtesy call. This meant that salutes would be fired by Cuban guns at Morro

Castle, at the entrance to Havana Harbor, and that the cruiser would have to return these salutes. However, the warship's guns had been put out of commission, as the ship was used only for training men in seamanship.

Before making the formal call, the ship borrowed from the Army a field gun with which to fire the salutes.

F.D.R. on vacation, interviewed by newsmen (*Wide World*)

CHAPTER 12

A Trial
Balloon

TWO DAYS AFTER ARRIVING at Campobello, *Amberjack's* destination, Roosevelt invited the correspondents who had followed him, and who had not seen him since his arrival, to spend an afternoon at the island cottage.

Nothing could sound more casual than this social invitation, but a demonstration of another facet of the Rooseveltian technique soon followed. It was new to public life and new to the press.

Before the day was over words had been unofficially spoken and unofficially reported—words that doomed an international conference and forcefully reasserted American independence of action and decision. Yet the President took no formal action and issued no formal statement on that day.

Here was the first of many events in which Roosevelt sought the co-operation of the press for actions that would be awkward or impossible within the limits of Washington's formal procedure. The technique involved a new informality for solving high-level problems. Roosevelt's use of this technique has been imitated, but seldom equaled and never improved upon.

In subsequent years the "little White Houses," his Hyde Park and Warm Springs residences, and occasional other places used for the same purposes, became a "third force" in the conduct of his office.

Campobello was the "little White House" on this occasion, and here Roosevelt showed himself to be the master of the "trial balloon." A trial balloon is a politician's idea launched for public reaction before he commits himself. By this means, much background, argument, good and bad reaction can be studied.

It is appropriate to remark here that the trial balloons and other techniques quickly won Roosevelt a reputation —not bothersome at all to him—of being less consistent than some other political leaders. He would blithely shift any course of action, if the public reacted negatively. But he had fairly and openly given notice of his intention to do just this—to make his political plays according to circumstances, as does a football quarterback, to whom he likened himself. He had given warning when he spoke at the White House of the economic crisis on April 19, 1933. He said:

It is a little bit like a football team that has a general plan of game against the other side. Now the captain and the quarterback of the team know pretty well what the next play is going to be and they know the general strategy of the team; but they cannot tell you what the play after the next play is going to be until the next play is run off. If the play makes ten yards, the succeeding play will be different from what it would have been if they had been thrown for a loss. I think that is the easiest way to explain it.

It seemed to many newspapermen and a few followers of sports "the easiest way to explain it," but it confused many of the old-line politicians of both major parties. Imagine the comparisons they made with the interpretations of the Presidency of Wilson or Coolidge or Hoover! Even Teddy Roosevelt never made so informal a statement.

It explained, however, the tentative pronouncement of a grave policy decision given toward the end of a leisurely afternoon at a vacation cottage on the shores of the Bay of Fundy.

June was coming to a close. The day was dull, with gray skies, in Eastport, Maine, across the bay from Campobello. Now that the cruise was over there came a period of relaxation. There were no more immediate uncertainties as to what we might be missing in news reports because of our physical distance from Roosevelt and no more real discomforts. The periods of rain and fog in isolated anchorages were past. But it was dull and depressing in many ways for the newspaper contingent that had trailed the President for three weeks on that fascinating but nerve-wracking cruise. Now all of us were feeling that the occasional seasickness and worst phases of the cruise would be preferable to this waiting period in Eastport.

Eastport was, in 1933—perhaps due to the Depression —among the most inhospitable and depressing towns any of us encountered in our travels with Roosevelt. It did not share the prosperity of resorts; it was too far north to be a yachtsman's port of call. Today, Eastport may have changed, but then it was simply a run-down fishing village. We had anticipated a rest period there in a neat hotel, but one sight and smell of the available quarters made us decide to hold *Mary Alice* and use her as a dormitory.

Finally, one day a dispatch boat arrived with an invitation from Mrs. Roosevelt to come to Campobello for lunch and an afternoon of relaxation. We had barely received her message when we were untying the dock lines and getting the motor ready so that we could cast off.

Mary Alice traversed the northern neck of the Bay of Fundy to an offshore spot, where we anchored; the island dock was too light to permit our fairly heavy craft to tie to it. Our "crew" rowed us ashore in the dinghy.

Mrs. Roosevelt, with Anna beside her, greeted us on the beach, and we walked up the path to the cottage. Since the cottage would have occasionally to house a large family and many guests, it was spacious and sprawling, but not at all like the palatial mansions we had sailed past during the trip; not like the "cottages" at Bar Harbor and Seal Harbor. Roosevelt, of course, had not visited here since 1921, but his mother, wife, and the growing family of five children had been regular summer occupants.

The cottage was, if my memory is correct, painted red with white trim, and it was situated on a low cliff overlooking the bay. Other buildings fanned out from the main house, but we did not enter them. On the first floor of the Roosevelt house were large rooms furnished with plain, practical, mostly chintz-covered furniture. The draperies at the windows were also chintz.

The living room opened into one or two sitting rooms and onto glass-enclosed verandas. Behind the cottage, there was a mass of evergreen trees. The view was mainly of the water, the gray-blue cold water of the Bay of Fundy, everlastingly overhung with cirrus clouds that frequently dipped low and became fog.

In the house we met the President, who was sitting and awaiting us, with a stack of metropolitan newspapers beside him. He was dressed comfortably in his favorite vacation costume of slacks and a worn sweater. He was not wearing his braces. No one could look more the part of a loafer than he did at the moment. In fact, until the rigor of repeated years in office, and repeated crises, began to show in lines in his face, Roosevelt appeared to be the most relaxed individual in the whole wide world. He seemed to be able to assume such an air at the drop of a hat.

The informality of his conversation seemed to indicate that there was nothing special about this day but the pleasure of a visit. He assured us that we "would miss nothing." "The news lid is on"; nothing would be announced to the agency reporters while we were at Campobello.

He began relating the story of this bleak coast, site of the first English settlement in what is now Canada; of the refugees in the time of the Revolution whose loyalty to the British Crown prompted them to sacrifice everything they had achieved in the Colonies to emigrate here; of the later days when New England "abolitionists" literally passed southern slaves northward via the "underground railway" to assured freedom in New Brunswick.

Roosevelt—always a brilliant storyteller—oriented us by pointing the directions to Maine on the west and Nova Scotia across the bay on the east, and recounted something of the feats of the older fishing fleets. He was most eloquent about the famous schooners that sailed as far as the banks off Newfoundland for their catches and then raced home to market. He showed us a new trophy, a model of the schooner *Gertrude L. Thebaud,* presented to him by a delegation of modern deep-sea fishermen from Gloucester.

The afternoon passed pleasantly. We were served a buffet luncheon, and afterward Roosevelt suggested a game of cut-in bridge.

However, play had continued for only an hour or so, when the President pushed back his wheel chair and said, "I think it might be more interesting just to talk for a while." He looked at his watch, and added, "You'll want to go back to your dock with the tide, which gives us about an hour more here." (We were amazed that Roosevelt, then probably the busiest man in the world, could take the time to keep up with the tide variations in Campobello.)

Within five minutes we who were invited to "talk for a while" realized the trap into which we had fallen. Roosevelt was off and running on a "conversation" that must have been conceived as spontaneously as a message to Congress. Etiquette of the day forbade us to take notes; we listened.

The President immediately made it clear that at the moment he was entirely preoccupied with the progress of events at the London Economic Conference, where Moley would have arrived long before the conclusion of this vacation cruise. No reporter present had the least idea what messages had come to the President by cable or mail, but some of the confusion at the conference was apparent in the newspapers.

In London were Moley, whose status puzzled everyone; Herbert Bayard Swope, former editor and occasional confidant of Roosevelt; and, of course, Secretary Hull, who had not planned on anyone complicating his responsibilities of statecraft. It seemed that no one knew quite what the United States advocated or expected, and the British had added to the confusion by proposing that the dollar be "devaluated" in relationship to foreign currencies.

Now, we could see why Roosevelt was disturbed, and why we had been invited over for this session. Roosevelt might be an internationalist, something of an Anglophile through family and friends, a cosmopolitan; but at this stage he was determined that the United States was not to be pushed around.

The President began gently by explaining that some way must be found to bridge the misunderstandings he saw existing both in the United States' attitude toward Europe and in the sometimes patronizing and erroneous view of the United States held by some European leaders. In fact, the Europeans for the most part were pledged to gain "concessions" from the United States for their countries, even though all but Finland had not paid past debts.

These countries simply did not realize, Roosevelt emphasized, that the European bonds were not held by the American Government or its agencies; they were owned by private citizens. The American investors had trusted the debtor countries as they did their own, and yet they had wound up with worthless or depreciated bonds at a time when they needed their savings most. He dwelt at some length on this feeling of resentment by the American public and furthermore indicated that he agreed with it.

He had accepted in good faith the proposal for this conference in London and had worked long and closely with Hull and the State Department to develop helpful ideas for Europe, with whose people he sympathized. Naturally, there should be some mutual accommodations to make debt-paying easier, and to increase world trade, such as the proposal for reciprocal tariff reductions.

Roosevelt's anger became more obvious. He insisted that the changing of tariffs could not allow the dumping of products by any cheap producer on American markets. The United States must not reduce the value of the dollar so that foreign governments could trade it at bargain prices in other markets. Roosevelt did say that the time might come when this devaluation would be to American advantage, but it was not beneficial to our own country in 1933.

When he came to that point he stopped talking, almost abruptly. He fitted a fresh cigarette into his holder and lit it. The speech was finished.

After a moment of silence, we asked a few questions and he answered them—but there was no need to ask Roosevelt's intent. He reminded us that the tide would soon change and that we should return to our boat. He remarked half apologetically that he had "talked too much."

Each of us looked from one to the other. We understood what we had heard but, for the moment, had not the slightest idea of what to do with it.

In foreign affairs—for that matter in domestic policy—this was a major story of the year. We were also operating under the injunction that the President is quoted only with his approval.

Finally one of us asked, "Is that for publication, Mr. President?"

"No," he replied, "it is off the record."

"Or for use without attribution?" another asked.

"We were simply talking about background," Roosevelt said. He smiled and then, after a pause, added, "Of course, if you were simply discussing this on your own, would you not possibly reach the same conclusion?"

Another commented, "Mr. President, you know very well that no one cares a whit what we think; we don't make the policy."

This was a minor crisis. The President had not authorized anything, and yet he obviously wanted to release these thoughts without taking responsibility for them.

"Well," he said, "how you handle anything you write is up to you. But isn't a Campobello dateline a pretty good hedge?"

At that, one of us said, "Thank you, Mr. President," in the manner in which newsmen ended the regular Washington press conferences, and we said our good-bys.

Aboard *Mary Alice* and on our way to Eastport, we were jubilant *and* worried. This story alone made the whole assignment worthwhile, but it could not be treated lightly. One word of denial by Roosevelt, when it was published, would discredit any reporter. Each of us got out paper and pencils and reconstructed the whole talk. We checked each other's version of it. The story had to be written, now that we were in possession of it; but if it was a trial balloon that would punctured tomorrow, at least we all would be holding the same string. My dispatch to *The Times* began without qualification or equivocation, "The Government of the United States will not agree at the London Economic Conference to devaluation of the dollar." The remainder of the story was a reconstruction of the conversation—without attribution.

The Times printed the story without even sending back an inquiry. Accepting the account without question demonstrated the faith editors have in their reporters on major assignments because, although columnists and feature writers can speculate without raising even a small cloud of interest, the public generally believes what it reads in the news columns. That is the great reportorial responsibility.

The story did hit like a bombshell; many European newspapers reprinted verbatim the American reports. In effect, it wrecked the London conference. The writers of these stories never saw the subsequent White House or State Department reports, but Roosevelt liked whatever he received.

It was an anticlimax on July 2 when, en route to Washington from Campobello aboard the cruiser *Indianapolis,* Roosevelt released the formal text of a message to London stating his decision.

Accepting second nomination, 1936 (*Wide World*)

CHAPTER 13

Wrapping up the Package

On September 13, 1933, there was a parade on Fifth Avenue that lasted all day and tied up mid-town Manhattan. A quarter-million persons marched in it, and the newspapers reported that two million lined the curbs to watch and cheer it. In the parade were delegations from labor unions, deputations of business groups, and hundreds of other organizational representatives.

This was the National Recovery Administration Day Parade, held without precedent and never repeated. Dominating the parade was the Blue Eagle, emblem of the NRA and symbol of the first recovery from the effects of the Great Depression. This was the American way of celebrating a revolution as dramatic as any since Independence—a revolution in which no shot had been fired nor even any individual sent to jail or away for exile.

The parade was a kind of exclamation mark in the rapid series of events, beginning with the legislation of the "one hundred days" and building into activity all over the United States.

Roosevelt had returned from his Campobello cruise to find that the price of wheat on the Chicago Board of Trade, barometer of the whole agricultural industry, had risen on June 27 to over one dollar a bushel, as price supports and controls began to take hold under the Agricultural Adjustment Act.

On July 9, he had been able to sign an agreement with cloth manufacturers under the Cotton Textile Code, part of the NRA, assuring better national working conditions for the industry. The manufacturers of cotton textiles voluntarily agreed to a code under the NRA establishing a maximum work week of forty hours, abolishing child labor and setting minimum weekly wages of twelve dollars in the South and thirteen dollars in the North. Many agreements were made voluntarily, because it was at last possible for industry and labor to agree to such contracts without violating the Federal anti-trust laws.

A few days later, on July 12, the government took a revolutionary step. Postmaster General Jim Farley put all postmasters under Civil Service and thus freed them from the patronage whip of politics.

In the final days of July an action by the Department of Agriculture established minimum prices for grain trading. These regulations broke the power of "short interests" which had periodically forced prices down in order to "buy cheap and sell dear" and to make artificial profits.

Finally, the Blue Eagle was pronounced the symbol for General Johnson's NRA. On August 1 it was hoisted over the thousands of factories, plants, stores and other businesses; and it was displayed in offices, where NRA codes were effective. For the moment it was the status symbol of business.

The remainder of the year 1933 was relatively quiet. There were, however, enough new developments, in both the domestic and foreign fields, to keep the reporters busy.

In the home field, the railroads, desperately in need of government help to modernize their facilities, agreed to set a ceiling of sixty thousand dollars a year on salaries paid to officers.

At the other end of the social and economic scale, the Agricultural Adjustment Authority was authorized to buy seventy-five million dollars in food and clothing materials for distribution to the needy. Of course, this purchase also helped the producers of these surplus materials.

Roosevelt became noticeably more relaxed in his press conferences, Cabinet meetings and receptions. His smile was broad and his laugh hearty, and when he was driven to the Rhinebeck Fair, in Dutchess County, and received for a "homecoming celebration" at Vassar College in Poughkeepsie, he relished the cheers.

For the moment, foreign affairs seemed more pressing than the domestic crisis, which was receding after a fashion. In October Germany officially withdrew from the League of Nations and from the Geneva Disarmament Conference. But the countermove was ready. On November 16, the White House announced the "recognition" of Russia, an agreement to make some arrangement on Russia's war debts to the United States, and assignment of Bullitt as the first American Ambassador to Russia since the days of the Czars.

The changing political scene was highlighted on November 10 by a public speech in New York that ended forever the close friendship between Al Smith and Roosevelt. Smith denounced the Administration for issuance of what he called "baloney dollars" and for staffing key positions with "inexperienced young professors."

Roosevelt chuckled when he read reports of this speech, but he made no comment. He continued his preparations to go to Warm Springs to spend a long Thanksgiving holiday among his young friends and protégés.

In December he lost the help of a friend more important to him than Smith. Secretary of the Treasury Woodin had tried to resign in the previous August, but had withdrawn the request when Administration critics interpreted first reports as a "break" with the President. Woodin's health was declining so rapidly, that his resignation was accepted on December 20. He died shortly after.

In the closing days of December, Roosevelt prepared to announce the appointment of Henry Morgenthau, Jr., as Woodin's successor, effective on New Year's Day of 1934. On that same New Year's Day, Roosevelt was vindicated for his work as former Governor of New York in crippling the Tammany machine; Fiorello La Guardia triumphantly took office as Mayor of New York City, elected by a coalition of reform Democrats and Republicans.

When the new session of Congress convened on January 3, 1934, Roosevelt sent a triumphant message. He declared that the New Deal was here to stay (true) and that recovery from the Depression had taken place (questionable).

However, his budget message that followed within a few days, asking appropriations for the fiscal year that would begin on the following July 1, was sobering. It estimated that Federal revenues for the forthcoming period would amount to $3,250,000,000 while expenditures for routine expenses plus the New Deal programs were anticipated at $10,500,000,000—three times the prospective revenues.

Cracks in the solid structure of support behind Roosevelt were beginning to appear, and these widened when, by executive decree, the government devalued the dollar to the equivalent of sixty cents in "old money." The official price of gold was raised to thirty-five dollars an ounce. Since gold could not be possessed legally, this action affected only the value of gold owned by the government, but it shocked business momentarily.

Next, the government, with Congressional approval, created the Federal Communications Commission. Separate from the NRA, this commission was given authority over all radio, wireless, telegraphic and telephone services. It later became a permanent branch of the government and today it also regulates the television industry.

The operation of the relief programs developed a minor crisis in the Senate in April, when the President nominated Rexford Tugwell for promotion from Assistant Secretary of Agriculture to Under Secretary. Since officials can be appointed or promoted only "by and with" the Senate's consent, congressmen were given a means of probing White House action.

Tugwell had not been subjected to any more criticism than the other members of the growing "brain trust." His personal and official conduct were above reproach. But in his climb up the official ladder he also had been named as director of youth programs in the relief field, as an aide to Harry Hopkins.

The conservative Congressional leaders were not yet ready to attack Roosevelt, but Tugwell made a good target. The critics included those who questioned relief spending and those who believed the reports that some Communist "fellow travelers" were infiltrating this program.

A favorite joke of the period featured Tugwell and Hopkins and the huge headquarters building, one of the ornate and now empty mansions built in another day on Massachusetts Avenue. Hopkins, already noted for his salty humor, finally had paid a call on Tugwell to see his operation. He was met by Tugwell in the great reception hall of the mansion. On the walls were gaudy frescoes, and on the ceiling was a mural which depicted nymphs and cupids disporting themselves. Hopkins looked around, and then remarked to Tugwell, "I'll buy a drink but I won't go upstairs."

Sometimes careers hinge on such anecdotes, but Tugwell weathered the storm. After an embarrassing delay of two months, the Senate finally approved the nomination of Tugwell by a solid vote of fifty-three to twenty-four. If the Senate had voted the day Tugwell's nomination had been sent to the Capitol, the margin of victory would have been the same.

Later that same month Hopkins published a report on the unemployment relief program of which he was over-all steward. He estimated that sixteen million Americans were being either directly or indirectly supported by relief.

Summer and the remainder of the year would have been a period of comparative quiet for the New Deal Administration, except that a first-class row developed around the fiery and opinionated General Johnson. The fight exploded less than a year after the great Blue Eagle parade.

It gradually became apparent that Secretary Frances Perkins did not like Johnson's hell-for-leather methods, in which he mingled threats and cajolery in speeches to industry around the country. Nor did she like his blue language. By this time it was a serious thing to be disliked by "Madam Secretary." Roosevelt thought highly of her, and she was growing in popularity even with those who had derided her appointment.

Another critic of Johnson who came into the open was Donald Richberg, a prominent and popular lawyer in corporate practice, who had helped to draft the National

Industrial Recovery Act, upon which the NRA and the Blue Eagle were erected. He had then become its legal advisor.

Richberg finally stated publicly with some exasperation that "the war on the Depression cannot be won by a single cavalry charge." The statement undoubtedly was made with Roosevelt's approval—itself a sort of "trial balloon."

After Roosevelt received some reaction to Richberg's statement, he broke the quiet of a Sunday afternoon at Hyde Park to announce the general's resignation and the appointment of Richberg to succeed him.

Johnson's dismissal came after Roosevelt had been forced to accept a resignation that he resented intensely. Lewis Douglas insisted on being relieved of the job of Budget Director, in public protest over the Administration's "failure" to live up to Roosevelt's Inaugural pledges concerning economy. This resignation really galled Roosevelt as he considered Douglas a valuable conservative member of his official family, and had stipulated that his post should be equivalent to Cabinet rank.

In 1934 the public witnessed the fading of the fresh bloom from the New Deal, but the interim Congressional elections, spurred by a wave of trips taken by Roosevelt, saw the supporters of his program solidly return to office.

However, many actions had gone into court for tests of their constitutionality, particularly cases concerning the Blue Eagle and the devaluation of the gold standard.

The new Congress convened in January, 1935, and started routinely; there was no radical legislation before it. In February the Supreme Court, still preponderantly conservative, gave the White House cause for encouragement: it upheld the legality of the dollar devaluation.

However, on May 27, the Court struck the New Deal

a body-shaking blow by ruling that the National Industrial Recovery Act and its companion measure, the Agricultural Adjustment Act, were unconstitutional.

These agencies immediately had to stop their activities, and lights burned late in government offices as attempts were made to pick up the pieces before the feared disintegration of the industry "codes" took place. Shortly after these decisions the President lost his temper and denounced the Supreme Court. But he could have spared his blood pressure.

Traditionally when the public has shown general approval of broad new ventures they survive. The Blue Eagle was wounded but not killed. Congress worked quickly to amend the law to meet the Court's requirements, and save the "voluntary" aspect of the laws.

Even before the amending was concluded, however, great forces rallied behind the program. The steel industry announced, within ten days after the Court decision, that it proposed to stand by the voluntary codes to which it had agreed under the NRA. The crisis evaporated.

Thus it was almost an anticlimax in August when, after months of committee study and debate, the Congress finally passed as law one of the most sweeping and enduring programs sponsored by the New Deal. This was the Social Security Act, which established provisions for unemployment insurance and old-age pensions, financed by payroll deductions.

On September 6, Roosevelt wrote an open letter to Roy W. Howard, publisher of a nationwide newspaper chain, stating (prematurely as it turned out) that the emergency phase of his Administration was completed, and that henceforth there would be a breathing spell. After what had seemed such a short time, the campaigning of another Presidential year, in 1936, was on the horizon.

The reassuring public statement of a breathing spell

came as a lulling influence in domestic controversy. But newspaper headlines followed soon after heralding the news of another foreign crisis precipitated by one of the dictators.

In October, Italy began its unprovoked invasion of the kingdom of Ethiopia. This action aroused much American sympathy and brought diplomatic protests, but there was no inclination to intervene. It seemed that a majority of Americans considered this another problem for the League of Nations. But the crisis indicated Roosevelt's foresight in starting the program to build a modern American Navy.

As 1936 brought Roosevelt's first term into the home stretch, there was hope in some quarters that the rising debate over New Deal programs was a sign of future defeat for Roosevelt. The tempo of legislation dropped from a gallop to a mere trot. All activity in Washington was concentrated on the task of getting a mandate for continuation of the New Deal. Roosevelt went off on a long cruise in the winter, and spent more and more long week ends in Hyde Park. However, these rest periods were deceptive. It was political hunting-time again, and his absences from Washington had the purpose of providing privacy more likely for political planning than for the apparent relaxation.

Instead of concentrating on legislative planning with the "brain trust," Roosevelt spent more and more time with Jim Farley, meeting with political lieutenants and allies, and studying the national mood.

In addition, he laid out the most strenuous travel and campaign schedule yet undertaken. Before election day he would visit every region in the Union.

In April, while all these plans were in a preliminary stage, Louis Howe, still the closest member of Roosevelt's political family, died. For a while the effect on

Roosevelt was so noticeable that his friends wondered if he would lose his vigor and his positive leadership. He made no effort to hide his sorrow, and demonstrated his high regard for Howe by an extraordinary gesture. Louis Howe's body lay in state in the East Room of the White House before it was buried.

And when the President turned to find a replacement, he chose an individual that he was least expected to. Harry Hopkins eventually was invited into the White House, both as resident and confidant, with the rather loose title of Assistant to the President. Until 1938, Hopkins also continued to be Works Progress Administrator; his rival Ickes, continuing as Secretary of the Interior, likewise grew more and more powerful in his role as Public Works Administrator.

In 1936 both of these men had become such controversial figures that many people wondered whether Roosevelt would jettison one of them as a means of squelching the growing criticism of public spending. He never paid heed to such reports.

At times, the revolution against the New Deal seemed to assume large proportions. Southern political leaders, organized by Senator Walter F. George, of Georgia, became outspoken critics of Roosevelt, principally for his invasion of States rights through the allocation of Federal relief and public works funds. Furthermore, although integration was not as yet an issue in southern politics, insistence upon equal opportunity and pay for whites and Negroes on projects financed by national funds was resented by the old guard.

In the more conservative elements of business, there also was a noticeable disenchantment, the biggest indication of which was the formation of the Liberty League. The League was not a political party but a movement backed by the business and financial communities. Also, there were rumblings of complaints from small business owners—shopkeepers, service agencies—about the paper work and records required by the new employment and Social Security laws.

When the Republican Convention met in 1936, the Republican leadership nominated Alf M. Landon, Governor of Kansas and a thorough-going conservative, as its candidate. The campaign became a contest between two diametrically opposed philosophies.

Landon hedged on farm relief but attacked every other phase of the Roosevelt program. However, he was not colorful, and his management was not of the highest caliber. He soon became the underdog fighting the old master, but he was encouraged both by published criticisms of the President and some of the public-opinion polls.

Roosevelt did not disregard the signs that encouraged Landon. He campaigned as though he were "running scared." Wherever he went, he emphasized the local benefits of his national program. He halted his train a dozen times a day for "whistle stops," as Harry S Truman later called them. He toured all of the rather widespread drought areas, issuing promises and directives for emergency relief action. He toured the prosperous farm areas to point out how much *better* off they could be in the future.

Across the country, he preached the benefits of the industrial codes under the NRA, and he filled his formal speeches with statistics of improved business conditions. He visited camps of the Civilian Conservation Corps now working in every major wooded area of the United States. Not a dam or public project went unnoticed from Tennessee to Oregon.

In New York City, the show of the year was the formal opening of the Triborough Bridge, a massive work over the East River uniting accesses to Manhattan, the Bronx and Queens—started and completed under the New Deal's Public Works program.

His campaign was an extended reiteration of the theme of "peace and prosperity." Even "peace" had an element of prosperity, as the great shipyards, which only a short while earlier had been overgrown with weeds, echoed with the noise of construction.

Yet in all of this picture there was the appearance of massive support for Landon. It fooled a number of groups, including both wishful thinkers and careful students of political trends. As late as October, gamblers gave Landon even odds to win.

The poll takers were completely befuddled. Those who anticipated a Roosevelt victory forecast a narrow one. *The Literary Digest,* a declining but still a leading national publication, predicted a Landon victory.

Seemingly fresher than ever, rather than fatigued by ceaseless travel and campaigning, Roosevelt returned to Hyde Park on the week end before Election Day.

News reporters covering the President at Hyde Park went out to the town hall early in the forenoon of Election Day to watch the President and Mrs. Roosevelt, accompanied by Mrs. Sara Delano Roosevelt, cast their votes.

The day passed quietly for the President, most of whose large family was gathered about him. The radio broadcasts carried occasional bulletins from rural areas where the polls closed early, but for the most part all was quiet. It should be remembered that then there was no television; no electronic computers forecast results.

In Hyde Park House there was some augmentation of special telephone service, connecting the President directly not only with the White House and his small offices in nearby Poughkeepsie, but also with the Democratic National Committee offices in Washington and New

York. Jim Farley waited in the command post in New York.

About nine o'clock in the evening, when significant results began to come in, Roosevelt invited the news reporters working in Poughkeepsie to visit his house. There they remained, phoning occasional bulletins to their newspapers until about midnight.

In the large living room, Roosevelt sat relaxed in an easy chair. "Holding court" in another area of the room was his mother, on a sofa which she shared with rotating groups of visitors. Marvin McIntyre handled the little "telephone room" and came to the President with bulletins as they were received.

The whole scene was quiet and not even charged with suspense for very long. There was simply no contest. Even that night with some western States not reporting at all, it became apparent that Roosevelt had a landslide victory.

In that evening, however, Roosevelt reserved his broadest smile for a report of a few votes in one election district. For the first time in his political life, from State Senator to President, he carried his own district.

On the following days, even Roosevelt supporters, with one exception, were overwhelmed by his showing. He had won forty-six of the forty-eight States, losing only Maine and Vermont. The one person not surprised was Jim Farley who, a week earlier, had given Roosevelt a sealed envelope containing exactly that forecast.

This was a triumph. Yet in some respects it was a requiem for the New Deal.

Roosevelt was no longer the imaginative young crusader preaching a new way of life for a desperately fearful and depressed country. He was the veteran leader, who had won the approval of the voters to carry on established policies.

His intimate aides were no longer the imaginative young men with ideas supporting his hopes and his promises. They likewise were veterans of the political wars wielding vast power in a great bureaucracy.

There was even some question as to whether the Roosevelt victory represented the "solid section" of the country—the established people with property, the responsible people.

More than one red-faced pollster justified the badly erroneous predictions by pointing out that "samplings" of sentiment had been taken primarily among "solid people." The implication was that Roosevelt's majorities came from the drifters, the shiftless and the unemployed whose living depended on relief.

Such speculations soon subsided, in the weariness over campaign arguments that eventually settles over the United States. But the battles to come would allay any fears that Roosevelt would become—even if he had wished —a "dictator."

Within a year Roosevelt's overwhelming, majority support returned by the electorate to the House and Senate would be conflict-ridden and divided. In addition to the Republican minority in the opposing ranks, there would develop a highly conservative bloc among the Democrats.

When he would attempt to reform the Supreme Court in 1937, opening the way to augment his supporters on that bench, the attempt would fail.

When he would attempt to "purge" some of the senior Democrats opposing him—notably Senator George— from the Senate, he would fail.

The year 1937 would bring a recession that would require more and more emergency action to "prime the pump" of the economy.

But before the next election in 1940, war in Europe would so envelop America's friends and enemies that the next election would be mainly fought, and won, on the basis of continuity for America's defense.

The New Deal was now the "old deal," and it was passing into history.

PART FOUR
Purely Personal

F.D.R. and Mrs. Roosevelt on the lawn
of Hyde Park House (*Wide World*)

CHAPTER 14

The Little
White Houses

THE FIRST PART of this book has been mainly concerned with the politics of Roosevelt and his circle; this last section deals with the personal—his homes, his wife, the man himself.

The "little White Houses" were unique in Roosevelt's era. They were without precedent and have not been duplicated since then. Hoover had a fishing camp on the Rapidan River in Virginia. Other Presidents have maintained retreats for quiet week ends, but all were different from Hyde Park House and Warm Springs, where Roosevelt took his work with him.

All Presidents have had permanent residences that they maintained during their periods in office, partly out of sentiment and partly in order to maintain political "roots." It is never good politics for a President to seem to settle down in the White House; he must keep a "legal residence."

Until recent years, however, the United States has not been considerate of its highest officeholders, despite the outward show of the White House, with its great staff, fleet of automobiles, private trains and planes and the other panoplies of position.

There have been only four really wealthy Presidents: two prior to Roosevelt, Washington and Hoover; and two after him, Kennedy and Johnson.

Both Thomas Jefferson and James Madison were so impoverished in their public service that after their deaths Congress bought their libraries as a form of aid to their families (from these came the beginnings of the Library of Congress).

Andrew Jackson mortgaged a cotton crop one year to pay his debts before leaving Washington to return to the Hermitage. Rutherford B. Hayes lived so economically that after leaving office he thought it necessary to announce publicly that he had not "profited" from the Presidency. Ulysses S. Grant spent his last year, suffering from cancer, writing with Mark Twain's assistance his memoirs, to provide an estate for his family. A recent biography of Woodrow Wilson reveals how, on his retirement from office, a group of friends created a large secret fund to purchase the house that he desired but that was beyond his means.

Franklin D. Roosevelt stood somewhere in the middle ground of wealth, as had Theodore Roosevelt—sufficiently well-to-do to suffer no obvious hardship. After his mother's death, in 1941, he bequeathed the Hyde Park estate, including the family mansion and the Memorial Library, to the government. And he did not survive office and thereby cash in on his position by writing as did "Teddy" before him, or Truman and Eisenhower after.

In any event, Roosevelt's possession of other ample residences established a new mode of life for the President, slower paced but comparable to Johnson's manner of commuting between the White House and the LBJ Ranch in Texas.

The two wealthiest modern Presidents showed little inclination to get out of Washington; it had already become their basic home. Hoover had established a house there in World War I, during his years of humanitarian service and his twelve as Secretary of Commerce. Kennedy had been in Congress for fourteen years—since young manhood—before he won the Presidency. Thus Hoover's fishing trips and Kennedy's visits to Hyannis Port and Palm Beach were vacation jaunts.

But to F. D. Roosevelt, Washington was a confining place to work. Thus the house at Hyde Park and the cottage at Warm Springs—and Campobello on occasions and the wartime retreat of Shangri-La in the Maryland hills in wartime—were essential to his need for diversity. All were synonymous with the White House in his activity as well as his relaxation. High-ranking officials, advisors and visitors were summoned to them as to the White House itself. Later, in wartime, with secrecy covering his movements, the public often had no idea where he was when public pronouncements were made.

Such a routine was much simpler in Roosevelt's first term than in the era that began in 1942 and increased the complexities of the Presidential office. They have never diminished. With the development of the Security Council, a world-wide intelligence service, the threat of instant warfare created by the atomic age, the "hot line" to the Kremlin—all of these have made it mandatory that the President be instantly available, any hour and anywhere. Even the Presidential staff has increased to include confidential aides always ready with special codes for world-wide communication.

In the campaign trips of Johnson in 1964, there was consternation in Washington because, while traveling at the expense of the Democratic National Committee on political trips, he economized by riding a relatively small jet plane not large enough to carry all of his aides. For only a few hours he did not have at hand the secret paraphernalia of his office. In contrast Roosevelt's out-of-Washington life seems almost pastoral.

Some description has been given of the Hyde Park mansion and the Warm Springs cottage, in which the President could read, dictate and confer in privacy not available in the White House.

The major problem away from Washington was the additional hazard to his safety. Every wooded area might conceal a "crank," and any desperately determined assassin might mingle with the groups whom the President saw in the neighborhoods.

The pulsating heart of White House business at Hyde Park was actually in a hotel in Poughkeepsie, the Nelson House, a twenty-minute drive from Hyde Park. Here the telephone and telegraph companies installed facilities linking the "temporary offices" on a permanent basis with the White House, with extensions to Hyde Park. The Secret Service already had wireless telephones in their escort cars. Rooms were set aside for the secretarial staff and kept in constant readiness by the hotel, which profited nicely by the extra business. Roosevelt's visits also brought to Poughkeepsie the unofficial train of correspondents, photographers and newsreel men—a real boom for the town.

At times, too, there was so little news of interest that the area profited from the feature publicity—about Vassar College, the golf course (reputedly third oldest in the United States), the Smith Brothers candy store and restaurant maintained chiefly as a memorial to the bearded brothers who discovered the formula for their famous black cough drops in its kitchen.

Even newspaper circulation increased: the Nelson

House newsstand raised its order for the daily *New York Times* from six copies to fifty, and the Republican *New York Herald Tribune* maintained an even higher level.

Roosevelt often joked—dryly and sometimes bitterly—about his Republican surroundings, which had long since reverted to normal. His representative in Congress was Hamilton Fish, Jr., most conservative of Republicans, and the State Assemblyman was Republican. At his first homecoming as President, there was no public demonstration in Poughkeepsie or in Hyde Park, although the summer group at Vassar College invited him to a reception and he was cheered when he visited the Rhinebeck Fair.

For newspapermen, the assignment was a repetitious chore, broken spasmodically by important visitors and unexpected events. However, the President loved his surroundings, and he and Mrs. Roosevelt could renew briefly the family associations. Their stay seemed to refresh them for their mutually busy and often separate lives.

There also was the Cottage. In earlier years, the Roosevelts had made a small decision of great importance to themselves—the purchase of a farm at the edge of Hyde Park Village named for its location, Val-Kill. This was the Cottage and it was just that. Very small with screened porches and a scrubby lawn under old shade trees, it was the antithesis of the great Hyde Park House. The only thing big about it was the massive outdoor fireplace for grilling. It had a pool where the President could swim in the privacy he relished, but even the pool would be called by today's suburbanites a pond. Those who touched bottom while swimming in it felt the grass growing there.

The Cottage was the private retreat of the President and his wife—a place where their children could go to play or to entertain their friends. It was convenient to Hyde Park House and could be reached by a route of back roads off the main highways, over which Roosevelt could drive safely and without public exposure in one of the small touring cars especially equipped for manual operation.

This was at a time before automatic transmissions were available on automobiles. All gears had to be shifted with a foot-operated clutch; both the accelerator and the brake were foot-operated. Automobile manufacturers already had created ingenious contraptions for people who could not use their feet. Levers were installed to enable drivers to drive completely with their hands.

Roosevelt had to keep the emergency brake locked while he started the car. He adjusted the hand throttle, declutched with one hand and shifted into low gear with the other. Then he had to put on the traffic brake with one hand, release the emergency, and finally let go of the clutch lever. To shift gears while driving he would brace his body against the steering wheel to hold the car "steady on its way" each time he clutched.

Roosevelt's driving, particularly in traffic, added several gray hairs to Colonel Starling's well-thatched head. The Secret Service pleaded with him to give up this self-driving, but here he was adamant. And who could blame him?

For this man who had been an all-around athlete for almost forty years, driving and swimming were the only forms of exercise remaining. He resolutely clung to them and probably drove more vigorously and with more abandon than he would have, had it not been such a challenge. F.D.R. never had a driving accident, though his children were involved in various accidents, and even Mrs. Roosevelt had a serious collision in later years.

In Hyde Park the President was senior vestryman of the small Episcopal Church which he attended, and where he had been christened. As a church official he was rather demanding. His clergyman once confided to reporters that when the President attended services, he shortened his sermon, because Roosevelt long ago had made it clear that he considered superfluous any exhortative talk lasting longer than twenty minutes.

Newspapermen saw little of the informal life of Roosevelt at Hyde Park because visits and calls with neighbors and friends often took place along private lanes off the Albany Post Road, which ran past the mansion's gates. He made—and kept—an agreement that reporters should be notified by the Poughkeepsie office of all official callers or special business if they, in turn, would not send prowlers or photographers into the grounds.

Thus the newspapermen's days often were spent tediously awaiting reports—never quite daring to go off on excursions, unless with the President himself. There were occasional evenings at Hyde Park House, or picnics at the Cottage, which Mrs. Roosevelt threw open to reporters, unless there was some special engagement made by her. Often there were invitations to movies at Hyde Park House, shown on the terrace after dinner with portable apparatus and films contributed by the newsreel companies.

Since Roosevelt was gregarious and would travel anywhere to visit friends, newsmen assigned to him saw much of Dutchess County east of the river, particularly Pawling. The town of Pawling has become known in recent years as the place where Thomas E. Dewey has his country home. However, in 1933 Pawling had not yet heard about Dewey. He had just begun to move up the political ladder with his appointment as U.S. Attorney for the Southern District of New York (New York City). His involvement in the "racket-busting" inquiries in 1935 pushed him into national prominence.

Pawling was best known locally then as the home of Lowell Thomas, the radio commentator, whose success already had provided him with an imposing farm, with a swimming pool and grounds on which he later constructed a private golf course. He was so independent that he had installed his own private studio from which he broadcast his regular evening commentaries.

Nearby was the house of K. C. Hogate, then the chief of the *Wall Street Journal*. After the first months of the New Deal, this financial newspaper opposed most of Roosevelt's programs. Thomas had organized an amateur softball team dubbed the "Saints and Sinners" (with 250-pound Hogate at second base) which played Sunday afternoon games for the benefit of the organ fund of a local church. Soon his team challenged the White House correspondents—a rather sad competition despite the agility of young John Roosevelt, who was "loaned" to bolster the team.

Not far away was the summer home of Henry Morgenthau, Jr., who, austere even with the President, marked his summer relaxation with a clambake prepared by a professional crew. The feast was complete with lobsters, clams, chicken, corn and other ingredients all prepared in sealed bags.

The only excitement in the serene life at Hyde Park came from an occasional piece of unexpected news. The news of people coming and going, the echoes of Depression and international crises kept correspondents at work generally for longer hours and more vigorously than in Washington. Roosevelt always took with him to Hyde Park some plans for news to keep his name alive in the press.

At Hyde Park on one Sunday, August 31, 1934, he accepted the resignation of Lewis W. Douglas, Director of the Budget, who thus protested the failure of Roosevelt to keep his pledges of government "economy," and appointed a successor. On another Sunday, there was a flow of news of such importance that *The Times* printed six different front-page stories from Hyde Park. No one could be so naïve as to believe that these occurrences happened spontaneously at a mansion on the banks of the Hudson River far removed from Washington.

It finally became a mark of prestige, or the lack of it, for officials to be summoned to Hyde Park for conferences or to be ignored. The same was true each fall season at Warm Springs.

The Warm Springs sojourn occurred only once a year, at Thanksgiving and two weeks following. Since the time period was shorter the visitors were fewer, but every visit was spiced with news and important callers. There was the same staff, and there were the same communications facilities in the earlier years, but everything was simpler—marked by drives over the sand hills, occasional picnics by the roadside and trips for newcomers to "Magic Mountain."

"Magic Mountain" was a hill with a mile stretch of road which presented an optical illusion that so frightened many of the local residents they would shun it at night. It was a simple thing but a pleasant joke which the President enjoyed playing on guests. He would drive them in his little car to the top of this hill and then halfway down the road. He would stop, put the gears in neutral and wait for the shock of amazement when the car started to roll back "uphill." The surroundings made the road seem to slant in the direction opposite to reality, and no amount of gazing and study could change the impression. Ickes became downright angry when he could not establish a reason for the illusion.

It was said that "the Indians had discovered it first," and that there had been a sort of shrine for mystic rites at the spot. The mythical Indians of early times were credited with almost everything we saw at Warm Springs. No one ever saw any Indians.

What correspondents did see, however, was one phase of Roosevelt's interest which those who knew this urbane man only in other surroundings would hardly have believed—his absolute dedication to rural development which in time probably accounted for his genuine admiration for Henry Wallace.

On his original farm at Warm Springs, Roosevelt had conceived the idea that farmers thereabouts might supplement their poor incomes by raising beef cattle for market—not the prize cattle expensively bred and fattened for prime beef, but a type of inexpensive range stock that could exist on the available grazing land.

One of the first points of interest to which Roosevelt guided visitors was a farm owned and worked by a native who, among others, had proved the profitability of this development. His cattle were not sleek and shiny, but rather scrawny; they undoubtedly would produce the type of meat used in canned goods. But they found a market, because Roosevelt had studied, experimented and proved that quarter-bred cattle could grow profitably on this land. He had bought the bulls that with the scrub stock had produced the crossbreed and now gave their service free to the farmers in the area. This contribution was very important to a countryside that was as poor as this worked-out scrub-farm area was.

Here in the older sections of the South it was customary for the natives to go "possum-treeing" regularly for part of their food supply. With the help of their dogs, and carrying lanterns at night, they would tree opossums, shake them down and take them alive. Then they would pen them, fatten them on corn like pigs, and eat them as a part of their regular diet.

On other drives, Roosevelt purposely led reporters along highways where gully washes beside the paved surfaces often had made ditches from six to ten feet deep in the soft clay. Whole sections of roads sometimes caved into the ditches. Speedy driving at night was extremely dangerous.

Actually Roosevelt was not interested in a bit of local highway, but he was dramatizing a broader interest—his preoccupation with erosion. He described what he had learned years earlier from Gifford Pinchot, later Governor of Pennsylvania, and a wealthy man whose hobby was conservation. Pinchot had once taken an expedition to the Gobi Desert to make motion pictures illustrating the extreme results of unchecked deforestation and droughts that had made this once fertile home of the dinosaurs a desert. Roosevelt seized upon every passing incident to develop some idea.

But there was another side to the Warm Springs picture, and its Georgia locale, that galled Roosevelt as much as his nonacceptance politically in Hyde Park. This was the bad impression which the political chicanery in Georgia gave the entire Democratic Party.

This feeling did not stem specifically from the subject of integration, which had not yet become a public issue or even a very common word in the American social and political language. It was still a matter of States rights. The Roosevelts already received a great deal of criticism in the North for their pointed actions in Washington, such as entertaining Marian Anderson or recognizing highly talented Negroes on an equal basis with Caucasians.

In Warm Springs, Roosevelt had fallen into the political sphere of Gene Talmadge, the Governor with the "red galluses" and backwoods oratory who held the rural vote firmly in his grasp—the vote of the poor white man because few Negroes could vote in Georgia in 1933. Furthermore, Georgia had the unit rule that loaded the legislature with rural members while limiting cities to one or two each. This kept "Ole Gene" firmly entrenched and held back urban development. This Georgian situation was a national embarrassment until the Supreme Court a generation later overturned its political system.

With his responsibility confined to national affairs, and Georgia securely in the Democratic bloc at that time, Roosevelt had to "take it." Even his most drastic reform projects were carefully tailored to his times. Only once in Georgia did Roosevelt make a point of his "Northern prejudices," as his views were considered by backwoods natives. When Atlanta completed, with Federal aid, a large housing project for Negroes, the President drove over to inspect it. Atlanta long ago established a high reputation for consideration within traditional limits for its Negro residents.

Before we finish this brief history of Warm Springs we should mention the Foundation and its blossoming into a national movement. It was not an institution in the ordinary sense of the word. It became a great program built upon a romantic idea largely through a publicity expert's skill in capitalizing on Roosevelt's name and position.

The little village was there long before Roosevelt discovered it. So were the springs, and their reputation.

The village's prosperity was sustained by the residents of a cluster of cottages. Activity centered around a general store and post office, built amidst the pine trees along winding streets that had occasional sidewalks but no paving. Some of these residents were prosperous people from distant cities who relished the climate for fall and spring vacations. A few of them were victims of polio who had been living at least part time in Warm Springs for many years.

Roosevelt "dropped into" this environment, for he had no part in creating it; his self-chosen task was to enlarge it, to create a retreat where children could undergo therapy, where specialists might learn new lessons and where studies of polio might continue. His own contributed property became something of an annex to the existing facilities. Not all of the older residents favored this scheme, but a touch of unpopularity, it is needless to add, never deterred Roosevelt from any plan on which he had set his mind.

The more massive movement culminating in the March of Dimes was born in the imagination of a famous public relations expert, the late Carl Byoir, who supplied the idea and the sponsor. His efforts turned a little Georgia project into a national monument for Roosevelt.

Carl Byoir had a wealthy client, Henry L. Doherty, an oil man, whose "public image" Byoir had been retained to embellish. His task was similar to that undertaken by Ivy Lee for the senior John D. Rockefeller.

In a search of good works that his client might sponsor, Byoir hit upon the idea of a vast campaign to which millions of children and adults might contribute dimes to help the victims of polio—the children. Out of this, after many intricate negotiations, came the March of Dimes, for which the first promotion expenses were underwritten by Byoir's client.

When Roosevelt accepted sponsorship, the campaign was launched in New York with a March of Dimes Ball. Mrs. Roosevelt, fully a head taller than Byoir, gracefully walked with him in the grand march at the ball. A photograph of this event held a place of honor on Byoir's desk until his death.

This anecdote is not told in a spirit of levity or to make fun of the promotion behind the March of Dimes. Byoir's sincerity, as well as his business acumen, was far too great for that; he simply had an opportunity that he used with imagination to promote one of his many interests for the benefit of children. This was the birth of the grand attack on polio that resulted first in grants to many scientific organizations for research, and finally in discovery of the Salk vaccine.

Neither was it a one-shot interest for Byoir, who also devoted his energy for many years as an advisor for the American National Red Cross. His love of children amounted almost to an obsession, which in later years pushed him to do things about which only a few of his friends ever knew. Despairing of having children of their own, Carl and Mrs. Byoir adopted after World War II three war orphans. This venture turned out so happily that soon they adopted three more.

By the time of his death, Byoir had personally helped six children; and, by energetic use of his public relations skills for the March of Dimes and the Red Cross, he had helped thousands more.

The mother and the wife of the President (*Wide World*)

CHAPTER 15

Mrs. Roosevelt

IN THE EARLY YEARS of Roosevelt's Administration a popular magazine printed a cartoon showing two miners in an underground setting. One was gazing past the other and exclaiming:

"Gosh! Here comes Eleanor. Now what is she doing—traveling around the world just making more trouble?"

The cartoon was reprinted in many places. Typical of Mrs. Roosevelt, she loved to tell people about it. Uninhibited, unself-conscious, she was as equally showered with loving compliments by millions as she was subjected to scathing criticism by others. The White House had never seen another First Lady like her. In time it became evident that she never thought of herself as being extraordinary in any way at all.

She liked democracy, she liked people and she crusaded for the underdog, after her husband became President with the same vigor as before.

She had five children who were substantially grown before the White House days, but she never had a house of her own where she could sit at the head of the table except the official "mansions" in Albany and Washington.

As a young woman whose overwhelming charm made one forget her homely features (about which she had ceased being concerned as a very young girl) she might well have hidden behind her famous and symbolic family name.

When she and Franklin Delano Roosevelt were married on March 17, 1905, the wedding was a notable event not because of the young lawyer who was the groom, but because of the family of the bride. It was an era of an older, quieter New York society, and Eleanor's uncle always created a stir. President Theodore Roosevelt traveled from Washington to New York to play the leading role in the wedding. Eleanor was the orphaned daughter of his brother Elliott, and "Teddy" gave the bride away. Newspaper articles of the time reported that the tall and very thin young woman already was noted for her welfare activities in New York City.

Thereupon she stepped out of the Theodore Roosevelt circle, in which Alice Roosevelt, the President's daughter, was attracting her own headlines by smoking cigarettes in public and wearing a red dress on at least one formal occasion. Eleanor simply disappeared in the ménage of Mrs. Sara Delano Roosevelt, who sent her son and his bride on a honeymoon trip around the world while she started construction of a dual house in New York City for the joint occasional occupancy of herself and the young couple.

For the next few years, Eleanor devoted most of her time to producing a large family. The years after John, her fifth and youngest child, was born, were years of development of Eleanor Roosevelt's public personality. She usually agreed with the reform policies of F.D.R., but in fighting reform battles she put her own mark of individuality on them.

When the F. D. Roosevelts entered the White House in 1933, Mrs. Roosevelt had shared twenty-eight years with her husband. They had spent most of them in the limelight except for the period of his paralyzing illness which likewise developed Eleanor's courage and stamina.

On the more pleasant side, she had shared his campaigning for public office. Washington saw her as an "old hand" after eight years of residence there as the wife of a secondary official. Because of the family's position and money they were able to be in the center of the capital's official and social life. She returned to meet both a host of faithful old friends and probably an equally large number of acquaintances who were now envious and critical. The Roosevelts had been out of Washington for twelve years, a fact which was unusual for an incoming President. Previous Presidents had moved into the White House from other offices in the capital; consequently, they were still a part of Washington's social life.

In her role as First Lady, Mrs. Roosevelt immediately attacked the stiff formality that still lingered in official circles, as in the case of her visit to Madame de Labouaye. She announced that the formal receptions and dinners would continue, but would be held to a minimum. She used her own telephone and often drove her own car to call or to see old friends. She even introduced square dances—at which she was a proficient "caller"—into the after-dinner entertainments.

The Roosevelt children all were adults, except for John who was seventeen, so their presence was limited to holidays and special occasions. The Roosevelts, in their leisure hours, therefore, had the same social freedom as other middle-aged couples making their own personal plans and renewing friendships with their contemporaries.

Perhaps surprising to readers in another generation is that Mrs. Roosevelt as hostess for her husband planned White House social life around names now considered to represent the truly conservative element of the United

States. Included were old friends from the Wilson years, some well known in government service and some not. They were either Washington residents or frequenters of the Capital scene. At the same time, the things that Mrs. Roosevelt did socially, such as entertaining Negro friends—of which much was made in some newspapers— were considered perfectly normal by this more sophisticated group if the guests were among their own cultural equals.

Among the close friends were Bernard Baruch, the financier, and Eugene Meyer, retired chairman of the Federal Reserve Board. Soon Meyer would buy *The Washington Post* and remake it into a world-famous newspaper after its virtual collapse under the ownership of Edward McLean, the husband of the flamboyant Evelyn Walsh McLean. Then there was Francis B. Sayre, son-in-law of Woodrow Wilson, whom Roosevelt appointed an Assistant Secretary of State. He also summoned to the State Department R. Walton Moore, noted scholar and diplomat. Moore was a native Virginian who had lived all of his life in the Washington suburban area of Fairfax County.

These men typified the Roosevelt coterie of close friends. In contrast, the Washington political and lobbying fraternity snatched at official invitations and hurriedly notified the newspaper society writers as soon as a prominent "name" accepted an invitation even to a cocktail party. Much of the later widespread "social" criticism of the Roosevelts sprang from this latter group, which might get cards to large receptions but never quite made the highest level of distinction—invitations to White House Sunday-night suppers.

These suppers were devised by Mrs. Roosevelt as the only possible manner in which to give the President occasional relaxing evenings among his friends with a semblance of the privacy he might have at Hyde Park.

Each new First Lady traditionally receives from the Congress an appropriation of several thousand dollars to finance changes in White House arrangements and decoration to suit personal family preferences. Most have waited until they had consulted with decorators before putting their personal stamp on the mansion. Mrs. Roosevelt, however, did not wait but moved ahead right after the Inaugural.

Striding briskly around the old house, she selected furniture from the storage rooms to furnish immediately a "family dining room" on the first floor. This area had been an anteroom off the office of the Head Usher. It could be served by the use of a dumb-waiter from the basement kitchen.

Here she started the famous little suppers, served to guests numbering anywhere from a dozen to twenty. All were invited informally, and it was strictly understood that the party was personal. No one was either important or unimportant politically in the order of invitations. The British Ambassador might find himself seated down the table from some young family friend who was merely a visitor in Washington. At this table, first names were used exclusively, except for the etiquette of guests addressing F.D.R. as "Mr. President." A typical main course would be sausage and scrambled eggs with waffles. At such a meal, waiters would serve a soup course and then pass first helpings of the principal course. Then chafing dishes and hot plates would be put in front of Mrs. Roosevelt, who would have guests pass their plates for second helpings.

Some critics seized on such little things to accuse the Roosevelts of breaking down White House manners and customs. But Mrs. Roosevelt did indeed appreciate the importance of official etiquette, as was evidenced much later the first time she was a dinner guest of the newly inaugurated John F. Kennedy. When the late President Kennedy escorted Mrs. Roosevelt into the dining room, he stepped aside for her to precede him through the door. She shook her head.

"You must learn," she said gently, "that the President of the United States always goes first."

In addition to the punctilious side of Mrs. Roosevelt there was another of genuine democratic feeling which permitted her without any qualms to organize picnics with outrageously mixed groups, to stand in line at bus terminals on some of her lecture tours and to put people of all types at ease with her.

At Campobello she once told a group an anecdote without seeming to realize how self-revealing it was. She was describing how charming the customs of Campobello were to her; she spoke understandingly of the pride of the native residents. In doing so, she recalled that an American couple had taken one of the cottages and settled in comfortably for the summer with a local couple as their house servants. The newcomers were quiet and desirable neighbors, but within a week the servants quit without notice or explanation. Mrs. Roosevelt's advice was sought by the visiting woman when she found that no one else among the unemployed persons would take the vacated jobs. Mrs. Roosevelt learned the reason quickly: on the first beach picnic arranged by the visitors, after the food was served, the help were told to eat by themselves.

"I felt so sorry for her," Mrs. Roosevelt added. "She had *never learned* that on picnics everyone eats together."

Probably much of Mrs. Roosevelt's ability to attract

attention during the White House years came from the fact that, although many women in her position might make such comments privately, she was just as ready to make them publicly. Thus what had been the charming frankness of a woman of relative anonymity became the character of "the wife of the President."

It was natural for her to accept lecture engagements which she kept without charging for her time; she could never resist a request to address an audience or work for a movement, if it appealed to her. And it was a natural thing for her to hold press conferences, just as she had been interviewed on a lesser level of importance for many years.

A woman correspondent was quoted around Washington as saying, "Mrs. Roosevelt doesn't hide her light under any bushel; if she had a bushel she'd burn it to add to the light."

When Mrs. Roosevelt accompanied her husband to the White House in 1933, she seemed to feel she simply had walked into an atmosphere no more public than that which she had known most of her adult life. She was a recognized advocate of "causes," a public speaker already greatly in demand and a friend of most of the prominent career women in America. Secretary Perkins was a close friend.

Her first press conferences consisted of the usual chaff, until the women correspondents attending them found that instead of being austere and reserved, she liked to talk. In travels with her husband, and even more widely on her own, she had seen the country and met large numbers of people. She had opinions and expressed them brilliantly on many subjects: the exploitation of women workers, the plight of families in the depressed areas and opportunities for youth. When she talked she spoke from firsthand knowledge gathered on many long trips, driving her own car, and accompanied by Malvina Schneider, her personal secretary.

Her influence on legislation has been exaggerated; what angered her critics most was that no woman in the country rose to enough prominence to be a counterfoil.

Mrs. Roosevelt did more than talk. When a private group refused to permit Marian Anderson to give a concert in its auditorium, Mrs. Roosevelt helped to transfer the concert to the Lincoln Memorial and arranged a reception in Miss Anderson's honor at the White House.

As invitations poured in, Mrs. Roosevelt ranged farther and farther in her lecture tours, and began addressing bigger and more important audiences. She signed a contract for a radio program in 1935, with some arrangement for the pay to go to welfare organizations; and she started in that same year her newspaper column "My Day." But during F.D.R.'s lifetime the only public office Mrs. Roosevelt held was as a volunteer Assistant Director of the Office of Civil Defense in 1941 and 1942.

Mrs. Roosevelt's column, which became outstandingly popular, was syndicated by an organization headed by Roy Howard, publisher of the Scripps-Howard newspaper chain, all of whose papers printed it. Howard became one of the severest critics of the Roosevelt Administration. He was asked at one time why, since he disliked the New Deal so thoroughly, he continued to use Mrs. Roosevelt's column. He replied that as a newspaper publisher it was his duty to give his readers both sides of political controversies and that he considered "My Day" to be the best of the columns interpreting the New Deal.

Prime Minister of England Ramsay MacDonald
at the White House (*Wide World*)

CHAPTER 16

Personal Diplomacy

THE ONLY FEAR that reporters covering Roosevelt ever heard him express was not concerned at all with developments in American politics. It came from the clouds accumulating on the world's horizons created by the twin dictatorships of Hitler and Mussolini. These situations caused him to take political risks that no other President less popular than his first election proved him to be would have dared.

Some politicians considered his actions reckless considering the certain repudiation by some American groups. Others damned him as an Anglophile. The strong feelings about foreign affairs shown in the 1930s seem in the 1960s remote and unreal, as more responsible American concern has moved toward clearer understanding of situations abroad.

Nevertheless, one cannot have a true perspective without realizing that in the 1930s many organizations—veterans, churches, community clubs—seemed to think that extreme isolationism was the ultimate test of patriotism. Oddly enough, these groups were composed largely of recent immigrant stock. Many leaned heavily on General Washington's Farewell Address, *misquoted* to leave the word "permanent" out of his injunction in 1796 against foreign alliances.

It is the considered opinion of this writer that in this field Roosevelt showed the most courageous side of his nature. He cultivated friends who shared his views and opposed powerful men who scorned them, and in doing so he risked everything.

Senator William E. Borah was the most powerful Republican voice for isolation. Before 1932, as chairman of the Foreign Relations Committee, Borah was able to kill every proposal—even proposals made by Coolidge and Hoover—which looked toward co-operation with the League of Nations or adherence to the World Court.

Even as a member of the minority, Borah easily led to victory the blocs that regularly thwarted attempts after 1932 to create some co-operation with European free countries, since all treaties require confirmation by two-thirds of the Senate.

Unfortunately, Roosevelt's most important supporters were New Yorkers—Bernard M. Baruch, Governor Herbert H. Lehman, Joseph P. Kennedy (whose son John was in 1933 a fifteen-year-old schoolboy), James E. Farley, and other comparable names—the great bulk of whom happened to be either Jews or Catholics of Irish descent.

Because of the whipped-up prejudices of that day, it was unfortunately easy to attack "Jews and international financiers"; and it was even easier, in debates on foreign affairs, to raise the specter of the engulfing power of Rome concerning Catholics. As a third force of prejudice, the poverty-stricken simply were suspicious of prosperity, corporate or private, and wished to find scapegoats wherever there were people with money. In some of the earlier phases of investigations of financial wheeling and dealing in the wake of the Depression, some of the financiers did

not help the situation. Although the New Deal repudiated these men, any alliance with the great banking and
industrial institutions which had important foreign connections was impossible.

These combined prejudices resulted in a basic problem
for Roosevelt: he was an American Protestant Gentile
with native origins shared by few of his fellow citizens,
and he was trying to face, with educated moderation, a
world in which his Administration must strive to serve
American interests.

The very coalition that had swept Roosevelt into office
made his task difficult. As a wholly professional politician
he realized that the overwhelming emotional support—
given to him as a protest vote—which elected him is the
kind most easily lost. The second election was a long way
off, and actions that would create whispered questions
would be more dangerous than any open opposition to this
program and his political future.

It was in this early period that he once exclaimed to
newspaper reporters, bitterly, that he done only the minimum to save the American way of life, to preserve a
capitalistic and democratic society for American citizens.
It is unlikely that any correspondent realized, at the time,
the risks Roosevelt was taking in the light of changing
conditions since World War II—changes which Eisenhower and Nixon helped to bring about as much as Truman, Kennedy and Adlai E. Stevenson did.

The election of Kennedy finally laid to rest a conflict
that had existed in American politics since Independence,
even though John Carroll of Carrollton, who signed the
Declaration of Independence, was a Catholic. Kennedy
finally demonstrated that a Catholic President was as
much an American as any other. But this achievement was
long in coming.

The Catholic-Protestant conflict had been at the heart of much of the clash between the cities and the rural areas of the United States. The rural areas were predominantly Protestant; the urban areas, due to their large section of immigrants—Irish, Italians and other minorities—from European countries, were predominantly Catholic. Among these groups the more rapacious graspers for power and money came into political prominence.

Roosevelt had the luck to appear when Irishmen such as Al Smith and Jim Farley took the risks to make their own leadership respectable, and when others such as Mayor Anton Cermak were cleaning up Chicago. But they had not overcome the aversion to Catholics in positions of national leadership in general nor an aversion to that vague thing known to untraveled Americans as Rome in particular.

This was the door Roosevelt started to open, perhaps with the assistance of a little push from his good friend, George Cardinal Mundelein, of Chicago. The Cardinal, along with Roosevelt's other friends who were Catholics, helped the President keep his foot in the doorway. Roosevelt became the first President to receive a high official of the Vatican, albeit in the informal circumstances of Hyde Park.

In October and November of 1936, a tall, dignified, aristocratic Roman prince visited the United States. His name was Eugenio Cardinal Pacelli. Having abjured the privileges which he had inherited by birth, he had become, at the age of fifty-seven, Secretary of State for the Vatican. Prior to the six years in which Pacelli had held this office in 1936, he had been a priest and diplomat who had spent the years of World War I on assignment in Germany.

He was a statesman and a scholar who spoke, read and wrote most of the major modern languages (including the American idiom). People variously compared him to both the geniuses and scheming devils in the history of the Catholic Church. Four years after his death in 1958, a book and a play would emphasize conflicts over his conduct face to face with the Nazis in World War II. By that time, he would have gone into history as Pope Pius XII.

The reporters covering Roosevelt during a visit to Hyde Park in the fall of 1936 were notified without advance warning that Pacelli would hold an audience—not a press conference—on his private railroad car in the yards at Poughkeepsie after lunching with the President. The White House rules, in return for this opportunity, as laid down by Marvin McIntyre, were that no direct quotations were to be printed and no questions were to be asked about religious or political subjects. All news accounts had to emphasize that this was not an official visit but a "courtesy" extended by Roosevelt during a coincidental visit by a distinguished Catholic leader to the Catholic community in Poughkeepsie.

Here, however, was one circumstance that rules could not control: first, the Cardinal was too shrewd a politician to make any quotable comments on American politics, and, second, he was so colorful that his visit to Hyde Park alone was a dramatic event that could not be suppressed.

Our group of correspondents had gone at the early hour set in the afternoon to meet the Cardinal, only to be told by a White House Secret Service man sent along in advance that he was detained. While we lounged in the waiting room of the old railroad station, we became aware of a gradually increasing noise outdoors, and went to see what had caused it.

There we saw an extraordinary sight for a small city that never turned out a crowd for the President or anyone else, of whatever political persuasion. It was a sight which perhaps evidenced the deft political craftsmanship for which the Roman Catholic Church has been distinguished for ages.

Poughkeepsie then was much more isolated from New York City and consequently was more rural than the modern city with its new complex of industrial development. It was noted as somewhat of a "Catholic center," because of the large variety of church institutions and schools established in Dutchess County.

The schools had been given, without public notice in advance, a free afternoon to see and honor Pacelli, and apparently word had been passed around the large Catholic section of the city's population as to when he might be seen. As a result, the long curving roadway visible from the station was lined with massed adults and children when the car bearing the Cardinal came into view some four blocks away. Pacelli thereupon did what was for him a perfectly natural thing, but we feared that Secretary McIntyre, who watched with us, might have a stroke.

The car stopped, and the Cardinal, dressed in the colorful attire of his rank, alighted. He walked the remainder of the way at a slow pace, gravely raising his hand in a blessing alternately to the right and to the left, and the closed ranks of those lining his path dropped to their knees when he was immediately in front of them, making a kind of undulating wave. The devout silence of the crowd was maintained until the very end of his walk when they began cheering and applauding.

At the station entrance, the tall Cardinal nodded to his escort that he had finished his duty, and the group closed ranks around him before he came to us. A few moments later, word was brought to McIntyre that Pacelli was ready to receive us, and we were cautioned that only a few minutes would be granted for the audience, since he was tired.

No one objected to such a reasonable request, but frankly we hardly cared about other restrictions; each reporter had already sensed that there was a story of major interest simply in the description of the little walk that had followed the Hyde Park call. We had, however, not seen all of the "picture story," and we still underrated the interest-development capacity of the man.

As we entered from the observation platform, we stepped into what might have been a portrait setting for a subject painted by Goya, against the background of the private chapel of some palace.

For a Cardinal to travel the breadth of the United States in a private car was of some interest, but the car itself added to the impressive story. It was in striking contrast with the cleanly polished but standard Pullman product in which Roosevelt traveled as President of the United States. This car had evidently been specially prepared by the Cardinal's church hosts.

Where green baize and plush marked the car we knew well, this one had crimson walls, trimmed with gilt. The windows were specially draped over their standard shades. An armchair as ornate as a miniature throne was provided for the use of His Eminence in receiving guests, and gilt chairs were provided for the guests. The small wall spaces were decorated with miniature paintings.

In this setting the unusual guest stood to greet our small party. His first gesture showed him to be a consummate politician. When he held out his right hand, the palm was upward in normal position to shake hands.

Two of our group were Catholics, and they knelt and turned his hand to kiss his ring in the normal obeisance of members of their church. The Cardinal smiled and as soon as the ceremony of greetings was ended, he laughed.

"Gentlemen, gentlemen," he said to his fellow church members, "I am afraid I must admonish you."

George Durno flushed with embarrassment and asked, "What . . . sir?"

Pacelli laughed again, and added: "You knelt with the right knee, as in church. That is only for God. For people, like me, the left is correct." Then, with the ice broken, he invited us to sit down.

The audience never became a press conference, nor was it a formality. It lasted for an hour. The topics included the baseball season recently ended, the grandeur of the Rocky Mountains—"unbelievable"—some comparison between the American public works program, then underway, with the old Roman achievements, comment on the high level of humor in American radio programs, *et cetera,* through an hour of talk rich in the American idiom.

It all was frankly confusing—this living picture of an austere dignitary of a remote hierarchy; he chatted and laughed and talked on a friendly footing none of us, either as church members or as reporters, had seen before.

When we departed, he gave each of us an invitation, which we knew to be sincere, to take any opportunity on a visit to Rome to call on him. If identification were required by his secretaries we were simply to mention "Poughkeepsie."

The visit of the Vatican's Secretary of State had received very little publicity during the weeks he had been touring the United States. This was deliberate for mutually understood political reasons. Now suddenly, in what appeared to be the most casual of circumstances, the event of this day alone probably served the purpose of the whole journey.

In our next visit with Roosevelt, he declined to comment on his own talk, except to say that he found the Cardinal enthusiastic over his own experiences in the United States, and that he was glad that members of the

Catholic Church in such numbers had been able to see a representative of the Vatican.

But as time passed, it became evident that much more than this had been accomplished; that we had brushed against a historic moment without knowing what its value would be.

Because of the prejudices of the day, Roosevelt could no more have moved in this direction with American members of the Roman hierarchy than he could have flown. It was a popular thing for politicians to turn out for the parades held on St. Patrick's Day and Columbus Day in cities with heavy populations of Irish and Italian descent. However, even in Washington, there was not an informal contact of any kind between the American Chief of State and the papal representative.

In the national capital, the Vatican had a mission, housed in a relatively new and imposing Massachusetts Avenue residence, comparable with the larger embassies. But this was not an embassy. Archbishop Fumosoni-Biondi discreetly maintained the churchly contact between Rome and American bishops, and exchanged social courtesies with the missions from "Catholic" countries. However, his duties and his life were private insofar as the American Government was concerned.

Within three years, when war flamed in Europe, and the obvious American interest in keeping contact wherever possible outweighed religious prejudices, Roosevelt had a friend in the Vatican. His caller in Hyde Park had been elected Pope on March 2, 1939. Within another year, Roosevelt was politically able to send to the Vatican a "personal representative," Myron C. Taylor, himself a prominent member of the Episcopal Church.

When Pius XII died in 1958, his obituaries noted "the personal relationship between him and President Roosevelt."

As the years of the Roosevelt Administrations passed, most heads of state, prime ministers and royalty, visited the United States, but no act of personal diplomacy was more important than the liaison made with the world's oldest "throne" on the eve of World War II.

Press conference, 1933 (*Wide World*)

CHAPTER 17

Press Conferences and the Press

ROOSEVELT'S PRESS CONFERENCES in the White House came to be known among newspapermen as "the best show on earth." Held in his relatively small office, without benfit of broadcasting of any sort, they became of utmost importance to the public as news sources, and to him as political tools.

Roosevelt began the Washington press conferences on a twice-a-week schedule the first week he was in the White House. He continued them for twelve years, and the printed records of them fill many massive volumes in the archives of the government.

In the years marked by the events of World War II they became less frequent. He once commented that he sometimes thought he should cancel them in wartime, since there was such a risk of exposing secrets inadvertently. Nevertheless, there is no record of his ever having made a security slip.

All Roosevelt had to fear, and all that he ever had to regret from this exposure, were the occasional evidences of temper lost and the consequent displays of it. He was a well-disciplined man, and a gracious one, but when he was angry he could be very angry indeed.

At the peak of his conflict with the Supreme Court— angered by the overturning of the National Recovery Act —he called the Court the "nine old men," and commented on their "horse-and-buggy" mentality. That was indiscreet, and it was bad politics. When the President finally sent to Congress legislation to change or enlarge the Court, and let him appoint some new members, he lost a lot of friends. Even loyal Sam Rayburn, Speaker of the House, turned the gavel over to a colleague and dramatically "descended" to the well of the House to excoriate the measure, contributing mightily to its defeat.

Years later Roosevelt showed the temper of war-frayed nerves in a press conference when he presented a German Iron Cross to John O'Donnell, of the New York *Daily News,* while taunting him for his and his paper's criticisms of the conduct of the war. The consensus was that Roosevelt was hitting below the belt; it was surprising in view of his general ability to absorb criticism, and even to laugh at himself.

It has been noted that the press conferences of previous Presidents were such in name only—rare occasions on which a President perhaps would answer questions submitted in advance in writing. Some Presidents feared them and some resented them.

It had been the fashion for many past Presidents to talk selectively with a few friendly editors or individual senior correspondents, when they had a project that they wished "interpreted," or when they wished to insinuate a viewpoint into public thinking. That practice had a long precedent.

Washington got its first newspaper, the *National In-*

telligencer, in 1801, when Thomas Jefferson invited his
friend, Samuel Harrison Smith, a Philadelphia editor, to
come to Washington and start a newspaper that would
interpret the Jefferson viewpoint. (And in Smith's wife
he inadvertently acquired the first Washington gossip
writer.)

In the Civil War, Whitelaw Reid, then a correspondent
for the *Cincinnati Gazette,* won his first prominence as a
newspaper correspondent in Abraham Lincoln's confidence. He was one of the men at Gettysburg who, on
the train returning to Washington, helped Lincoln turn
the notes of the Address into a rounded little manuscript.

Horace Greeley, whom Reid finally succeeded as editor
and owner of the *New York Tribune,* was the oracle of
the Republican Party of his day.

By the time of the Hoover Administration, the relatively small but influential public that wished to know
what really was happening in high politics had learned
to read selectively the dispatches of a few correspondents:
among them, Richard V. Oulahan, of *The New York
Times,* J. Fred Essary and Frank Kent, of the Baltimore
Sun; Paul Y. Anderson, of the *St. Louis Post-Dispatch;*
Arthur Sears Henning, of the *Chicago Tribune;* Paul
Wooton, of the *New Orleans Times-Picayune,* or the
columnists Walter Lippmann and David Lawrence,
among others.

The staffs of the news bureaus worked hard, but always
on the periphery of the news, with little access to the top.
This was reserved for men such as those mentioned, whose
reputations were largely built on their admissibility to
private offices, invitations to select dinners, or rare mem-
berships in such clubs as the Cosmos, Metropolitan or
Burning Tree.

Suddenly all of this was changed, because Roosevelt
not only instituted the regular press conference, but his

example opened comparable doors to specialist reporters covering the departments. The public, even the readers of the hostile press, never realized its debt to his opening of these doors.

Roosevelt had a number of close friends in the newspaper world, but it is difficult to recall a single instance when these friends obtained a fact or viewpoint not given to their competitors. As time passed, many news writers or commentators became labeled as opponents or defenders of the Roosevelt Administrations, but the material they published, if and when it was exclusive, came from side sources.

Naturally, and it should be emphasized, the holding of press conferences did not make all the news available to newspapers and their readers. Sometimes the readers were misled, and sometimes news or the emphasis on certain points was distorted in the press conferences. But with one hundred or more seasoned reporters attending a normal White House press conference (or any other Washington press conference for that matter) open to all kinds of questions, a slip of the tongue or a misstatement could not live for long.

For the first time, it was pointed out by the astute old observer, Sir Willmott Harcourt Lewis, Washington correspondent of *The Times* of London, the Roosevelt Administration gave to the American public a semblance of the British practice of "question periods" in the House of Commons.

In Commons, as most American high school students may know, the question period is a ritual. Since the Cabinet members normally all are members of the House, or are represented by their Parliamentary Secretaries, ordinary members may file questions, which cannot be disregarded. There are established question periods. Naturally the answers may be occasionally declined, or the replies

may be evasive. But at least the questions are aired publicly and may be discussed after a formal reply has been
given to each.

Much the same purpose was served in the original
Roosevelt conferences, although the setting was far different and the answers generally were given only for indirect
quotation in the press. But at least the questions were
asked by a group of men as well informed about political
problems of the day as members of the House of Commons were about their own.

Finally, as the system slowly became more workable,
with both the reporters and the President patiently contributing to its development, the press conference
reached, prior to 1941, a pre-eminent place in our system
of government.

It did bring into the language, unfortunately, the
phrase "off the record." Soon everyone, from the divorcée
being interviewed by a society columnist in the Blue An-
gel to the ward heeler talking to a police reporter, was
preceding answers to inquiries with the phrase, "off the
record," thinking thereby to make their words sound more
important—and more likely to be printed.

Before the extreme tensions of the office and the added
burdens of war leadership began to fray his nerves, Roosevelt put on a superb performance in his press conferences.
At the same time, like most great actors he always was
palpably nervous and ill at ease just before each of his
"performances."

In Washington, where Roosevelt's press conferences
allowed no pictures and no broadcasting of any sort, the
President held them exclusively in his own oval office. He
seated himself at his desk, with his back to the windows,
facing the men who stood before him. Behind him, in
standards, were an American flag and the blue Presidential flag. Members of his staff or occasional guests—once

the guest was Winston Churchill—sat on sofas under the windows. After the doors of the office were opened to admit reporters, the President would play with his cigarette holder, arrange and rearrange papers on his desk top, perhaps finger one of the many souvenirs there, such as a little cotton donkey, speak over his shoulder to an aide, or exchange a self-conscious joke with reporters already lined up in the front row. The men immediately in front of the desk were the representatives of the news agencies, with some space reserved, by mutual consent, for a few older colleagues who did not see or hear too well.

The signal for the start of a press conference would be a loud call, "All in," from the office doorkeeper.

Here again, as in so many phases of the White House operation, a certain informality belied the tight security measures. The etiquette of such proceedings also created a greater feeling of distance between the President and the reporters, even though he came to know some of them very well. (One of them, John Boettiger, became his son-in-law for a while, as Anna's second husband.)

Every man and woman in the room—for women reporters were just beginning to appear in numbers as regular correspondents, as differentiated from writers of women's news—had been screened by the Secret Service and the FBI. Each held a card that had to be produced on request, not only at the White House doors but at the gates of the grounds. Prior to the security classification of passes started in World War II, this was the highest pass card in Washington.

Newspapermen, in phrasing their questions, always addressed Roosevelt as "Mr. President," or "Sir," but within a matter of weeks F.D.R. had mastered a wide range of first names and delighted in using them. More importantly from the public and newspaper standpoint, it soon became apparent that no reasonable question was "off limits," although it might not evoke a straightforward answer.

The normal press conference began with whatever announcements the President wished to make at the moment. It soon became clear that some of these statements were saved especially for the occasion. Later, as political controversy grew more intense, the White House would attempt to smother bothersome questions at the start by announcing such important news that these new issues would dominate the conference and the news reports.

After the announcements, the first question period was given to the inquiries of the agency correspondents. Since these questions were national or international in origin, they generally covered a wide range of interests. Then the "specials" would take their turn. The President's knowledge of detail always was a source of wonder. Because he did his own very thorough newspaper reading and was briefed well by his staff, he could discuss most regional or local problems that came up.

Most of the broad Administration programs were first outlined in these press conferences, or subjects previously announced would be amplified.

At a later date, the lend-lease program was first thrown out for discussion at a White House press conference. Occasionally the "off-the-record" replies were more illuminating than the indirect answer that could be attributed to Roosevelt. Because he established a high degree of reliability—allowing for a few marginal cases of politically expedient answers—these replies gave valuable background on current affairs.

In his answering or parrying of questions, Roosevelt displayed the very opposite of a "poker face." It was almost essential to watch his expression to understand the real meanings of some of his replies. His mobile features expressed everything from deadly seriousness to irony to boredom to anger. However, at the conclusion of each press conference, marked by a reporter's "Thank you, Mr. President," he was smiling and apparently relaxed.

If the news was "hot," there was a moment of bedlam, while the news agency correspondents literally raced to their private telephones always open to their offices. In the meantime, Henry Kannee, the stenographer, usually took a post in the lobby, with his notebook, to clarify what had been said on a specific question if any reporter was in doubt. Roosevelt, however, never authorized the issuance of transcripts of his press conferences.

If the news was of bulletin nature for the wire services, the President would be able to see within a minute or less the first reports as they clattered back on the tickers in the press secretary's office. In my several years of White House reporting, I never knew an instance wherein corrections of press conferences were subsequently issued or when the President reconvened a press conference to amend what he had said.

No member of any sizable news bureau assigned to the White House carried sole responsibility for all Washington reporting of the President's activities. Some press conferences would fan out into a hard day's work for a number of men in the same office, their assignments ranging from Capitol Hill to the Departments. Each was sent to check, amplify or follow special leads to stories introduced in the press conferences or uncovered by extemporaneous questions.

Somewhat similar and yet different in tone were the press conferences held out of Washington. The differences were due mostly to their smaller size and the resultant informality. The atmosphere is different when less than a dozen interviewers can sit comfortably and ask questions at a leisurely pace. These "homey" press conferences, as Missy LeHand termed them, were held under the same rules, and questions and answers often were as rough as in Washington. Those of us with publications dedicated to the national interest were selfishly happy to have talks freed of the local-interest notes.

The conferences at the "little White Houses" differed both from the larger ones held in Washington and from the unscheduled talk at Campobello (discussed earlier).

One such conference at Warm Springs, on Roosevelt's first return as President in November of 1933, probably indicated for the first time the scope that Roosevelt foresaw, and eventually realized, for the Tennessee Valley Authority. It had one result of arming his critics with more evidence of what they denounced as his policy of "creeping socialism."

Remember that the TVA was first authorized as a flood control and fertilizer-manufacturing project, with some preliminary preparations for installation of secondary power production facilities incidental to flood control. The original assumption was that if such power were produced it probably would be sold to existing private power companies in the area. They could buy the available electric power and transmit it to their customers, while saving their own higher production costs.

On a rainy afternoon, reporters met at the announced hour for the press conference, in the sitting room of the President's cottage. Behind him sat Mrs. Roosevelt, busily knitting. Other chairs were occupied by Marvin McIntyre and Henry Kannee. Speaking without notes and seeming to have made no special preparation for the meeting, the President first answered the few questions asked by reporters. Then he settled back, relaxed in his chair and affixed a cigarette in his holder.

Roosevelt started to talk about his hobby of developing

backward farm areas, citing work and experiments he already had begun at his own farm before it was given to the Foundation. He said that in broader terms such work needed two types of development: flood control for the great valleys of the country and cheap electric power available to every farm for the best modern agricultural efficiency.

Then he moved to his main point: that it might not be economical for private power companies to undertake such a vast project. He was sure that in the long run complete rural electrification would be profitable, but could the power companies make such large investments from their stockholders' capital when profits might be long in coming? he asked.

In his remarks, the President quoted George Norris, the famous elderly "liberal Republican" from Nebraska who had sponsored TVA and for whom the principal dam later was named. He cited Sweden as an example of one country that then had for a quarter century required that every new dwelling in the country be constructed completely wired and equipped for electricity.

Could we afford to wait longer?

Actually, what Roosevelt was saying was over our heads, but he was prepared for that. When the "conference" ended, McIntyre "happened to have" copies of a detailed paper prepared by Norris and printed—or buried—in the Congressional Record.

Later, when the first panic and fears of the Depression had subsided, these background news conferences became a political issue. The principal charge was that Roosevelt "used" the press conferences for his own purposes.

This was true to a large degree: he did make news. But reporters covering Roosevelt and alternating on other assignments as well had a simple explanation that was based on close observation.

All political candidates and party spokesmen wish to use the press—the term in this sense includes all information media. That is why they make speeches, hurl charges and sometimes try to invent situations for debate. This once was called "publicity." Now it has the more general name of public relations. It actually is provided for in our Constitution, with the stipulation of "freedom of the press."

The main complaint of the opposition—with recurring comparable parallels in more recent years—is that in this instance they were pitting inferior skills against a master of the art. In the two elections of 1936 and 1940 Roosevelt smothered his opponents, although they tried two entirely opposite approaches to beat him. Both battles were fought primarily through the press and radio.

Alf M. Landon, the Republican candidate in 1936 (a man of unquestioned integrity), backed strongly not only by his party but also by a dissident group, the Liberty League, which included Al Smith, suffered ignominious defeat. It was he who carried only two States, Maine and Vermont, as predicted by Jim Farley.

Landon campaigned for a return to the years that were past. Roosevelt beat Landon by a personal public relations campaign, skillfully managed by Farley and handled in its publicity aspects by Charles Michaelson. Roosevelt's campaign created news. He talked and talked and talked. When he passed through Kansas, he even stopped for a conversation with Landon.

This was "using the press" with a vengeance. It was "making news" that built Roosevelt's image as a champion of the people. In that year—to reveal a confidence no longer important to keep—*The Times* and its correspondent assigned to cover Landon held many worried conferences. *The Times* was, and is, dedicated to giving equal prominence to major opponents in all campaigns.

In 1936 it was leaning over backward, because it still supported Roosevelt editorially. But it had to overplay minor news to find things to report about Landon. Sometimes *The Times* sent out its own reporters to develop features that might be tied to the reports of Landon and make him seem more important. It takes a lot of work to be fair, and even more when a giant is overwhelming a pygmy.

In the year 1940 Roosevelt was again attacked for using the press; what was worse he had defied all precedent and custom and was running for a third consecutive term. He believed he had good reasons for this campaign, and he had the loyal support of his Washington team—of doubtful vote-pulling value—but not much else. Even a law of his own collaboration, the Hatch Act, laid criminal penalties on the use of Federal employees in political activities.

Some surveys showed that ninety per cent of newspaper circulation was opposed editorially to Roosevelt. Many of the most popular radio commentators openly slanted their reports against him. And Farley had left the fold.

The Republicans had their most glamorous candidate in generations, Wendell L. Willkie, who burst out of his Wall Street law office in a campaign of liberalism and with the slogan "One World" for a rallying cry. Arthur Krock received part of the credit for the Willkie boom, which swept through the Republican Convention that year.

Roosevelt looked over his political assets and liabilities and changed his whole posture from that which he had taken in the Landon fight. Through the publicity media he took his campaign right to the people—"using the press." He campaigned gently against Willkie, who supported much of his own program, and left the few dirty punches for his close associates to throw. (Harold Ickes labeled Willkie "the barefoot boy from Wall Street.")

Seeing the press rallying behind Willkie, Roosevelt almost complimented him with the derisive label of a "me, too" candidate.

By 1940 the special correspondents regularly assigned to the White House had long since scattered, except one. I had been assigned abroad in 1937, but due to a series of circumstances was sent back to the White House for the 1940 campaign, in a year when my newspaper removed its support from Roosevelt. One might have expected a hostile atmosphere.

But there was no hostility, largely because of the policy of *The Times* that strictly separated its news reports from its editorials. The editorials warmly praised Willkie; the news columns carried faithful reports of the dispatches from the campaign train, the White House, the big-city rallies and the "whistle stops," with the comparable quotations of speeches, estimates of crowds and other detail just as they had in 1936.

For the most part other newspapers did the same. More than the public realizes, the American press, except for its dirty fringes, interprets "free press" even beyond Thomas Jefferson's injunction to mean "free and fair."

During a press conference on Roosevelt's campaign train soon after *The Times* came out for Willkie, Roosevelt twitted me for my publisher's change of heart. I asked how it felt to be on the other end of editorial criticism. The reply was, in substance, as follows:

"If the newspapers report what I do and say, I am not concerned about the editorials or the columnists."

And of course, the "fireside chats" were still strong ammunition.

There have been many clichés used by Presidents from time to time in describing political events—the "great debates," "times of crisis," "moments of decision." Many catch phrases like these popped up in the years Roosevelt was in the White House. But the plain fact seems to be that he never overestimated a political crisis (although he underestimated some), never confined his political debate to one issue or one man, and he always acted and talked as though he *knew*.

Roosevelt always had an air of such confidence that some of us who were in close proximity to him often were asked odd questions by intelligent friends who were sincere in their fears. Had his affliction upset his mental balance? Was there a streak of megalomania in Roosevelt? Was he bluffing about his "disregard of criticism" to hide some weakness in his character or mentality?

Our denying knowledge of such afflictions often did not seem convincing to those who asked the questions. They could not believe that their criticisms and fears of Roosevelt were based solely on his ability to outsmart his opponents longer than former Presidents had. It is difficult to reduce to simple terms the multifarious weapons he used. Roosevelt employed every straightforward, intelligent (or clever, if you will) publicity resource open to the President. He covered over and over all of the issues at stake. He traveled incessantly, and he took his local news with him.

Frequently Roosevelt took real political risks to ram points home. Particularly was this true in foreign policy, where the nation's approval of his opposition to Nazism and Fascism never quite overcame the public aversion to his recognition of Soviet Russia.

The President and Mrs. Roosevelt went to some pains to raise the dignity and prestige of the "fourth estate" in Washington, not through the singling out of favorites, but en masse. From a social standpoint—an important aspect—the press always has been given a more respected place in Washington than in most other world capitals, but always on a "mingling basis." They were welcomed as "side guests" at large official functions, seldom given an equal place in special dinners at the White House, and only invited as "friends of the President" when entertainment involved some political skulduggery.

In the spring of 1934, the Roosevelts gave a garden party in honor of the press corps and later established annual receptions in honor of the corps. The guest list of state dinners began to be sprinkled with the names of prominent newspapermen, not as reporters but as equals of diplomats and statesmen. The same courtesies were extended to reporters for picnics at Hyde Park and outings at Warm Springs.

The sincere warmth of Mrs. Roosevelt's personality added to the better relations between newsmen and the White House. On one occasion when the mother of a bachelor news correspondent died, and the funeral service was held without publicity or fanfare, the correspondent learned only afterward that the Roosevelts had sent flowers, and that Mrs. Roosevelt had attended the services.

On the following Sunday the reporter went out for an afternoon drive alone, to think about the readjustment in his life, and returned to his apartment about six o'clock in the evening. As he passed the reception desk of the apartment house, the clerk excitedly called out for him to telephone the White House immediately. This was not too unusual, because there was a standard procedure for notifying White House correspondents when unexpected news announcements were to be made. He returned the call.

The operator on duty, however, did not have a notice for him, but said instead, "Oh, yes, Mrs. Roosevelt has been trying to reach you for hours!" She rang an extension and gave the correspondent's name. Mrs. Roosevelt said: "Oh, thank you for calling back. I was thinking of you this afternoon, and Franklin and I would like, if you wish, to have you come in for supper—that is, if you are not engaged. We're just a little group."

Thousands of words have been written about Mrs. Roosevelt. Some have been laudatory, many critical. But such evidences of consideration one remembers with affection.

On another occasion, a correspondent was about to be married and go on a brief honeymoon, when Roosevelt suddenly announced plans to go off for a holiday on *Nourmahal,* while the White House party would remain at Coral Gables, Florida, at temporary headquarters in the Miami Biltmore Hotel. It may seem strange to some readers, but in a conflict between one's own wedding and a major news assignment, the assignment takes precedence.

Word got around of the correspondent's predicament, which was solved by the President's intercession. Credentials and passes were arranged for the bride-to-be to board the special train and to ride it to Miami. The President's cruise, lasting more than two weeks, provided an undreamed-of honeymoon period, broken only by light daily working routine. The bride and groom returned to Washington on the special train.

Roosevelt sent word on the train that he would like to meet the bride. When he met her he puzzled her by remarking that now, as the wife of a newspaperman, she must be "the milkman from Omaha." He hastily explained to the embarrassed young woman that she could become her husband's best critic. She must in the future play the role of the average reader of his stories, once defined by Melville Stone, long chief of the Associated Press, as that milkman.

Perhaps here, too, a personal reminiscence will help illustrate a little-known side of Roosevelt, what might be termed his tenacious thoughtfulness. Others might be equally gracious, but, unlike Roosevelt's, their gestures would often be shallow protocol.

I had been continuously on the White House "beat" until Inauguration Day in 1937, when *The Times* decided that I should be reassigned. By this change they got a fresh outlook in the White House and broadened my knowledge as a reporter. There was an opening in the London Bureau, which was offered to me; I accepted it, and the departure date was set for the end of January.

Word reached Roosevelt of the change. Soon there came an invitation of a kind different from any of our prior engagements. The President specifically asked my wife and me to tea in his office at 5 P.M. on an early date. We arrived for tea to find only the President, waiting with McIntyre and Missy LeHand. It turned out that he wanted to tell us some things about the political situation in London, for my information, and to chat with my wife about life in that city.

It was the first occasion that we realized he thought of either of us as persons, as distinct from faces. He went into some detail in discussing public figures I might encounter and was equally solicitous in giving some homely hints about London living to my Eleanor.

At the end of the visit, he asked Missy to remind him to autograph a portrait for us, and he ticked off three names of people to whom he wished her to write letters of introduction that might be helpful to me. One of these was Colonel Murray, the retired British statesman.

On the following day, a White House messenger arrived with a packet containing one of his favorite photographs, the first official one of him at his White House desk, and the letters of introduction on White House note paper.

We sailed abroad. In London my wife and I became

busy. We talked several times about the letters of introduction, decided that they were interesting souvenirs, and
put them away in a keepsake box. We decided not to
identify ourselves as "presenters of letters."

Two months passed. One afternoon I was at my work
in *The Times* bureau, when a call came for me. I answered, and a gruff and burry Scottish voice rasped at me:

"Hurd, this is Murray. Where the hell have you been?
Franklin has written three times asking about you."

A "fireside chat" (*UPI*)

CHAPTER 18

Fireside Chats and
Hell on Wheels

ROOSEVELT'S "USING OF THE PRESS"—his ability to make news—compensated in part for the growing antagonism of the press toward him. It was, indeed, the image that F.D.R. created of himself which kept him in office. That image reached the people through the press, but even more it was delivered by the President in person, from the first days of the New Deal to the end.

On the night of March 12, 1933, Roosevelt went on the radio to "report" on his plans to the public.

An estimated forty million Americans grouped around their radios to hear him, listening intently despite static squeaks and the frequent necessity of fiddling with the dials. They heard the voice and the opening words that became a historic trademark: "My friends . . ." Upon hearing this voice, the overwhelming majority became immediately convinced that this was a friend, their friend, in the White House.

The only word to describe the reaction was "mesmeric."

When the President invited individuals to write to him about their problems, they did! More than forty thousand letters poured into the White House. Each one received a reply over the President's signature.

All of this effect was created by voice alone. There was no television. No one could see the speaker until newsreels taken at the broadcast were processed and rushed to the motion picture theaters. The Roosevelt presence added to the impact.

Then the public saw the Roosevelt smile, the old-fashioned pince-nez on the bridge of the formidable nose, and the informal soft-collared shirt, which Roosevelt introduced to replace the presidential starched collars.

The feeling created by the broadcast is difficult to analyze. The first chat evoked a response which might be compared to that of President Kennedy's first Inaugural, or Johnson's first appearance after Kennedy's assassination.

That night President Roosevelt won the affection of America. He was not a frontiersman born in a log cabin nor a common man come to Washington to fight for his fellows, but he gained their devotion. This President was well known as a wealthy, cultured aristocrat, and he made no attempt to disguise his background. He spoke with a broad *a* and had not a trace of mock humility in his bearing. He even discarded the dissembled "we" for the personal pronoun "I."

Of course, the broadcast was not spontaneous, nor off-the-cuff. Its simplicity was meticulously planned. A band playing "The President's March," one of John Philip Sousa's great compositions, opened the program. An announcer introduced Roosevelt with one line, "Ladies and Gentlemen, the President of the United States."

The "fireside chats" were superb theater, but good theater would not have sustained interest as Roosevelt radio appearances did for nineteen more times during the remaining months of 1933. He told progressively more of what he planned to do and reported on steps taken to implement past promises. He gave periodic appeals for support and occasionally made scathing remarks about his critics.

In the following months and years, as the list of his critics grew and the costs of recovery programs sometimes overshadowed their immediate results and the Federal debt multiplied, the favorable response diminished. But people still listened, and engagements were broken, if necessary, to hear him—or parties were hastily organized for the same purpose.

In fact, the "fireside chats" came to connote such a cozy form of personal report that, when the President spoke to the nation after the attack on Pearl Harbor in 1941, he felt it necessary to explain that this broadcast was much too serious to be considered a "fireside chat."

Nevertheless, in these earlier broadcasts, it was not very important what each individual subject might be; no talk ever was confined to a single issue. Subjects ranged from general reports of new laws to specific descriptions of the NRA, from the "good neighbor" program for Latin America to welfare and labor needs. Sometimes, with the nation as his general audience, Roosevelt spoke specifically to organizations like the Boy Scouts of America jamboree, the American Legion convention or the Civilian Military Training groups.

What was important was that the President created the effect of a friend visiting in his listeners' homes. Unimaginable work went into his speeches to convey this effect, including many drafts on special sections by specialists in various fields, detailed editing by the gifted Judge Samuel Rosenman and considerable technical advice from radio specialists including Harry Butcher, then resident vice-president in Washington of the Columbia Broadcasting System. Butcher's advice was technical, not political. (Butcher in those days often played golf with a neighbor who was an unknown Army major assigned to staff duties in Washington; later this same officer, when he became General of the Army Dwight D. Eisenhower, took Butcher to Africa and Europe as a special aide.)

Even after the panic of the Depression subsided, Roosevelt still compared favorably with the top names in radio like "Amos 'n' Andy," "Rudy Vallee," "The Lone Ranger" and "The A. & P. Gypsies." He might have gone down in the history of his era as "the radio President," but Roosevelt also showed from the start of his Administration that he planned to *see* and to be *seen*.

The American public had long become accustomed to —and to some degree wearied of—the traditional candidates for the Presidency who barnstormed the country seeking votes; and the victors who thereafter shut themselves up behind closed doors until the next election.

According to the cynics, Roosevelt simply kept right on campaigning. According to Roosevelt the White House and Washington appeared to be "headquarters" for menial chores; his real job was reaching the people. And throughout his years as President he never changed.

When the Warren Commission report on the assassination of President Kennedy was published on September 28, 1964, it noted that in Roosevelt's twelve years in office he had made approximately 400 journeys totaling 350,000 miles. These statistics mean that he made 400 trips in about 625 weeks, despite tight restrictions in World War II. During those years he made some trips which were longer than any previously, but the number dropped sharply.

At the end of the President's first year in office, interviewers asked his secretary, Marvin McIntyre, if the President's medical advisors were not concerned about the effects of so much travel on his health. Marvin seemed shocked by the question. He replied, "But he likes to ride on trains."

Furthermore, it may be added, he liked to ride in motor-cades; he liked to give speeches; and, even in the blister-ing hot weather or pouring rain, he seemed to enjoy spending whole days in automobiles, preferably with the top down or with only the protection of the uncurtained top of a touring car. ("Bubble tops" were yet to come.)

One recalls the distaste which numerous travelers had for overnight train rides prior to air-conditioning—a dis-taste for the perspiration mixed with soot and dirt that filtered through the screens of open Pullmans. But even on Roosevelt's longest train trips to dry prairies where the weather had added a final blow to the agricultural depres-sion he did not seem bothered.

When the farmers and businessmen in the smaller cities and towns saw the President on the rear platform of his train, or seated in his halted motorcade while he spoke a few words to them, the dust and sweat on his own face brought him closer than anything he could possibly say. And yet, despite the inconvenience and the discomfort of such trips, Roosevelt always did say something of im-mediate interest and importance to them—a remark on local conditions carefully culled by his staff from their information sources or from direct interviews with local personalities.

By 1933 most of the leading railroads had developed some of the modern features of "crack travel" before the mounting competition of airplanes, buses, and trucks had skimmed off the cream of the freight revenues. The Cen-tury, the Broadway Limited, the Super Chief—among others—were by-words of luxurious travel. But their luxuries were not for the President. Their lightweight construction ruled them out. The Secret Service demanded that the President's train be heavier and relatively safer than the deluxe trains. Automatically this put aside such developments as the articulated trains whose cars did not jolt with every stop and start, the diesel and electric locomotives specifically designed for the new trains, and the air-conditioning systems built into them.

Furthermore, the President went many places where service was not available for the newer equipment. One remembers an overnight ride between Pierre, South Dakota, and Fargo, North Dakota, over rails no longer used for passenger trains, where the speed of the President's train had to be held under twenty miles an hour. The batteries failed to receive enough charge to keep the lights bright, or to operate the electric motors that worked the flush toilets and lavatories.

The President's "private car" was a fiction. No such car was owned by the President or the White House; he rode in the borrowed "work car" of the president of the Baltimore and Ohio Railroad, among the most modern of its type but many years old, and not air-conditioned until later. Building of the car Magellan—armored for safety and up to the minute in comfort—would come only to protect the President against the possible bombing of tracks in wartime. For his trips, the White House used a Presidential seal on demountable clamps, attached to the vestibule of the old private car.

This car was almost as much the President's home as his rooms in the White House. Its vestibule seated from six to eight persons; two drawing rooms and a compartment provided sleeping quarters for his personal party. There was the luxury of a small private bathroom. A dining room seating eight was amidships, and ahead were a galley and pantry, plus sleeping quarters for two attendants.

Such cars had been the last word in status symbols for millionaires because of the great cost of keeping them in service through payment of excess fares wherever they rolled with their owners; they provided convenient and reasonable travel quarters for railroad executives. For extended work by a President they were ridiculous. For news reporters traveling on the assignment, they were simply another focal point of coverage.

In 1964, it was important campaign news when the candidate made a great point of occasional days of "whistle-stop" appearances, using hastily assembled trains for short jaunts through the countryside, to reach junctions faster than they could with motorcades.

These side trips were considered quite adventurous. But there was no presidential business actually conducted on them, and they were not really "whistle-stop" tours of the kind last practiced by Truman. Times had changed, both in the improvement of air travel and in the lessening of the President's financial problems.

At this writing the President of the United States enjoys a salary of $100,000 and a $50,000 annual travel and entertainment allowance (both subject to income tax), plus a special untaxed allowance of $40,000. But when on official business he travels by jet (in Air Force Number One) or via a fleet of helicopters, the Air Force renders no bill to the White House. What this means came to light in the 1964 campaign when the Democratic National Committee was charged $2,200 *an hour* for the jet rental for Johnson's political trips.

In 1933, the President was paid a salary of $50,000 a year, which was not bad, with higher purchasing power and lower income taxes. But his travel and entertainment allowance was $25,000 and there were no free train rides for Presidents, a rule which still holds true today. The practice goes back to a ruling by the Interstate Commerce

Commission made in the Taft Administration to stop
"dead-heading" by politicos.

In that era of railroad development, free passes had
reached a point where almost anyone with a little political
pull carried a national railroad pass in his pocket; if he
were influential enough it could be used to cover large
parties of friends traveling with him. The railroads had
themselves started this mild form of bribery, but it was
now swamping them. It accordingly was ruled that *no
one* except railroad employees thereafter could be carried
free. Incidentally the rule had been instituted for the
airlines, but that was long before the government itself
began operating the biggest air fleet in the world, as a side
line to military business.

The only item of expense not paid for out of the President's pocket was for the use of the special train car. The
Secret Service insisted on this car at Federal expense
after one hectic experience of trying to assure the safety
of Coolidge when he decided to save money by traveling
as a drawing-room passenger on a vacation trip to the
Black Hills in South Dakota.

Otherwise, the President's travel expenses became staff
exercises in efforts to keep him from bankruptcy. On his
trips, Roosevelt normally had to buy from six to eight
tickets—for himself, Mrs. Roosevelt or other family
members, and for two or three actual staff members.
Newspapers were billed for the transportation of their
representatives. The Treasury Department paid for the
Secret Service agents. Usually other government departments were "tapped" for the expenses of personnel loaned
to the White House.

Thus in pinchpenny luxury the President toured the
country in what was euphemistically described as "The
Presidential Special Train."

Surrounding the train, however, were such planning

and safety precautions as the country had never known, and an unparalleled record for safety. Only once was this train ever halted unexpectedly, when its automatic safety brakes locked and stopped it abruptly on a winter night in South Carolina. Secret Service men, railroad guards and newspapermen poured out of their quarters while floodlights were turned on and minute examination of the train was begun, mostly for evidence of sabotage. It took an hour to discover the cause: a huge jack rabbit, evidently blinded by the locomotive's headlight, had been struck by the engine precisely at a point where its body broke a small valve that tripped the emergency braking system. Fortunately, the President was not thrown out of bed.

Although Roosevelt was by temperament informal, let there be no misapprehension that visitors or newspapermen wandered in and out of his car at will, or that this became an informal club for everyone aboard the train. What the public saw, or the thousands of political visitors, whenever the train made one of its thousands of stops, was almost casual in appearance. But, like the casualness of the "fireside chats," all was carefully planned.

Whether the Presidential train rolled across the continent, or merely journeyed overnight from Washington, D.C., to Hyde Park, thousands of men and scores of services were involved to some degree. Each stop, whether for political reasons or for changing engines, was plotted to the minute; and the area was scouted in advance by Secret Service agents.

All rail traffic was shunted from the tracks to be used for six hours in advance. In that interval responsible railroad men would walk and inspect each yard of rails, looking for breaks or possible causes of accidents. Switches that might be maliciously or carelessly opened were

Hell on wheels (*Wide World*)

"spiked." All parked trains or cars were removed from immediately adjacent tracks lest they give cover for plotters. In the crowded East this was an inconvenience to railroads but a chore they gladly assumed, because they were proud—very proud—of a record of almost a century in which no train ride had ever killed or injured a President.

In the more remote reaches of the country, Roosevelt's trips often involved intricate schedules over smaller lines without duplicating sets of rails. We occasionally wondered how many thousands of persons fumed without knowing the reason why their trains were halted for hours, or why the train crews gave no reason for these delays.

In addition to the track and route precautions, the Presidential Special always was preceded by a dummy train, called a "pilot," consisting of an engine and a few coaches. It made the run as a safety test for the real train in case something had gone wrong, a switch had changed or a cracked rail had gone undetected.

All supplies put aboard the train were checked by security agents before delivery, even the water for drinking. Thousands of gift parcels sent by well-meaning but unknown admirers never got aboard the train, but ordinarily were destroyed.

If this sounds like excessive care, or an exaggeration, remember that Roosevelt and his entourage traveled in the dark shadow left by Giuseppe Zangarra's assassination attempt, which was a very recent event. In some ways, the memory became worse when it was established that the gunman was a madman. Had it been a gang plot the gang could have been destroyed. But obsessed individuals are always to be feared more than calculating or hired killers.

The Secret Service detail and their aides meeting the train at Presidential stops slept little and never were at ease. Colonel Starling, chief of the White House detail, had an air of impregnable calm, but he walked in a shell of concentration throughout each trip. He literally "sweated out" each casual stop when jostling crowds swept to within a few feet of the President who encouraged them, as a politician, by holding out a hand to shake theirs.

It was the age-old contest between politicking and security, with some but not much co-operation from the President. Even so, the guards and Presidential secretaries screened in advance every politico scheduled to board the train, gave him special directions as to what to do and how to behave, often more bluntly than the President would have liked.

In the meantime, operation of the train proceeded under the direction of a vice-president of the railroad over which it happened to be traveling. It was run by specially picked crews—with a second trustworthy veteran to replace immediately any active crew member who might fall ill or come under suspicion.

On his first major trip out of Washington, to Boston in June 1933 en route to board *Amberjack II,* the Secret Service invoked all of its special authority to forbid the President to greet the public on the city streets. This angered Roosevelt, particularly because it involved Boston where he was not popular and he feared it might cost him future support by his friends.

When the train arrived at the New Haven station, uninformed persons must have thought all hell was breaking loose. The old station was suddenly transformed to avoid the usual necessity of transferring the President from the train to an automobile and then driving by a circuitous route out through the yards to a public street.

As the train approached the station, Secret Service agents and police appeared with specially drilled workmen. They took down a section of gates and fence separating the public rotunda from the tracks, removed massive doors connecting the rotunda and the main station and made an opening from the waiting room directly to the street.

In an isolated area of the station, the President was placed in a plain black limousine, preceded and followed by unmarked guard cars. On signal, a motorcycle escort came out from places of concealment and joined the cavalcade. With sirens screaming, the cavalcade sped directly through the old station to the street, jumped the curb and turned onto a pre-policed route over which it traveled at maximum speed, out to and beyond the city limits.

Later in the day, Roosevelt profanely expressed anger over these arrangements, and was mollified only when the Boston papers and political leaders generally approved of these precautions. But a similar routine never happened again.

Even with all of these security measures lavished on an "earth-bound" President, Roosevelt worked under what would seem later to be primitive conditions. Yet to come were radio telephone circuits over which conversation could be scrambled or cipher-coded mechanical telegraph machines or electronic equipment capable of putting the President in immediate and confidential touch with any official anywhere, at home or abroad.

As a result, thousands of detailed plans had to be devised for travel communications and an army of people enlisted. On every scheduled stop of the President's train there was a switchboard for his use, with open communication with Washington. The telegraph companies had parallel message equipment on hand, which also served the press. A Western Union representative—for years Carroll Linkins—rode the train to give advance warning of arrivals or changes in schedules to those waiting for train stops with the service equipment. E. W. ("Doc")

Smithers, the special White House telegrapher whose job dated back to Grover Cleveland's second Administration, sent the confidential messages at these stops. He was custodian of the secret code book occasionally used for cipher transmission, particularly between the State Department and the President.

Finally, the Army Air Corps supplied airplanes and pilots to carry couriers with bulky documents from the President's office, and back to Washington. These couriers usually met the President's staff twice daily.

In this period before the great breakthroughs in communications spurred by World War II, the only new communications device offered by train, telegraph and telephone was the amplifier for public speaking installed on the platform of the President's private car.

There was not even a tape recorder for his public remarks or interviews. In thousands of pictures of the President making impromptu talks, there appears a dark-haired man, with heavy-rimmed eyeglasses, almost leaning on the President with a look of benumbed concentration. This man was Henry Kannee, the skilled stenographer, who under indescribable conditions could take accurate shorthand notes with such fine-lined accuracy that other superior stenographers could transcribe them.

In the Pullman car ahead of the President's private car, compartments and drawing rooms were turned into combined living and working quarters for the traveling staff, equipped with typewriters and mimeograph machines.

Third from the end of the train was the dining car, equally convenient to the other members of the party up front and for service to the Presidential car. Never a fussy eater, Roosevelt often liked to choose his food from the larger regular train menus, a fact which accounted for the "policing" of all supplies put on board. (When Presidents eat at banquets or other public functions, they appear to be served as is everyone else, but with rare exceptions the Secret Service insists that all their food and drink be separately prepared.)

Life in the other cars of the train was geared to the tempo of each trip—its destination, stops and the persons either riding as guests on the train or those received aboard for brief visits.

The bulk of the passengers consisted of White House newspaper correspondents, news syndicate photographers and the crews handling the newsreel sound cameras.

The office, club room and life-center of the train for these reporters and recorders was the club car, and, in the late hours of the night when meal service was ended, the dining car. The club car had the only shower bath on the train, except for the private car, but its water supply was strictly limited, for on normal trains a passenger taking a bath was a novelty.

Pullman cars never were designed for continuous occupancy, especially in their ventilating facilities. So the porters used air "purifiers," which really were only masking agents for stale smells. For hours after such spraying the train would smell of synthetic carnations.

Activity was almost constant. Throughout the long days and evenings, news was always breaking, and when the late-night hours arrived there were countless advance stories to be prepared, or features ordered by editors to be completed. Activity did not stop entirely even then.

At every stop, news reporters and photographers, who could not parade through the President's car, had to leave the train, often fighting their way through crowds of spectators to the rear of the train, make their notes and their pictures, and then fight their way back to the open cars.

More than once a nearly marooned reporter had to be dragged over the railing of the private car as the train was pulling away.

Even in the "quiet watches of the night," much of this coverage continued. Even when the President was not appearing on the platform, during service stops for the train, the tail end had to be covered for "protection." This was a euphemism meaning that if an intruder tried to board the train, or someone threw a bomb, the reporters had better be there. Correspondents might seem to their readers to be writing exclusively of high statesmanship, but their editors also expected them to remember the lessons most had learned as young police reporters.

But then, as now, there was irony in this whole security program. Despite all the precautions to protect the President, and the work by newspaper (and now radio and television) correspondents to cover his every public move, he eventually meets crowds face to face—on streets, in railroad stations, at air terminals, everywhere—and insists on doing so. That is the almost imponderable problem that caused J. Edgar Hoover to state publicly in 1964 that ultimate protection of a President's life might involve creation of a "police state." As for the correspondents, they no longer can "cover" the President in the older sense of the word. When he travels by airplane, they ride on another one. When President Kennedy was shot, his political cavalcade was so long that no newsman or cameraman saw the event.

In this train life, relaxation took virtually only two forms: cards or, after the repeal of Prohibition late in 1933, drinking. The drinking was very moderate. Even ordinarily convivial newspapermen had learned long ago that drinking and around-the-clock work simply do not mix. But the card games became marathons to while away the hours between urgent assignments. It was a rare hour of the day or night when tables were not being used for poker and bridge, as restless men took the places of others with work to do, or with rest to get.

Cards, too, were the principal relaxation on the President's car, after dinner dishes had been cleared from the table in the little private dining alcove. Here again a game helped to relax the President and his aides between hectic station appearances, particularly if his schedule called for late-evening stops and he must remain dressed in clothes and braces.

Roosevelt did not play often with the press contingent, although periodically he sent individual invitations to some of the reporters who gladly accepted them and enjoyed the games. More often than not, the President used his moments of relaxation to report confidential matters to his staff. At the same time, few news correspondents wished to be in the position of hearing such conversations; thereafter they would have to respect such confidences if in their ferreting for news they came upon the same information from other sources.

Since Louis Howe never traveled with the President, Early and McIntyre rotated in the secretarial chores. Both were excellent poker players. Dr. McIntire was a fair one. "Pa" Watson was good company, and a good loser. Roosevelt had an excellent card sense, but he would rather lose and laugh uproariously at a bluff tried and lost than play consistently to win.

Even in the field of poker, however, Roosevelt sometimes used these games for important political maneuvering. Once it seemed that he held in check in this way what might have been an otherwise irreparable breach between the highly sensitive, ruthless and ambitious pair of Ickes and Hopkins.

As the power of these two men grew, and the appropriations for their respective fields of public works and relief made each of them stronger, they became mutually jealous. Finally it was public knowledge. The situation was worsened by their respective partisans or opponents and fed additional fuel by the irresponsible columnists.

Since Roosevelt could not solve the problem by firing either of his trusted aides, and a public statement denying the feud would only have seemed to confirm it, he used one of his long "inspection tours" for an experiment in public relations. He invited both of them to accompany him.

For nine days Ickes and Hopkins were aboard the train or with the President on his motor trips to visit construction projects, dam sites, forestry projects and the other miscellany of the New Deal recovery program. At every opportunity he played up the importance of Ickes and Hopkins as his guides and counselors in these works— and he played poker with them almost every night.

How much Ickes and Hopkins guided or counseled the President at this time was a matter of confidence between the principals; but the feud, if it existed, dissolved and the public was fed such a spate of news and pictures of the men co-operating publicly that reports of it dissolved.

Roosevelt often was accused, sometimes with reason, of turning his "inspection tours" into political junkets at the expense of the government. (What President has not been?) But what is political? And what does the public wish of its President? Mostly they want to see him. And when every appearance is a painful physical effort, they appreciate it all the more.

It is true that political shenanigans reached a high level; whole delegations would travel from far places, in an effort to persuade the President "on his next trip" to receive some local figure aboard his train. This was especially so in "politicking years." Every effort was made to accommodate these requests, and in turn the White House unblushingly used the flattery of an invitation aboard the train to win local support or to smooth political feathers ruffled by refusals of patronage. Also, the President could take care of some small debt due a local figure he would never see or be seen with in Washington, knowing that the publicity would be limited to a local area.

Countless politicians of the middle and late 1930s were pictured in what photographers termed the "set piece," on the rear platform of the private train, standing alongside the President and just above the Presidential seal on the railing of the car. Some were rushed aboard for this picture at a short stop and rushed off by an efficient White House staff without having an opportunity even to ask a question in the midst of cordial greeting, let alone get a promise or receive a word that might be quoted later as, "Confidentially, the President said to me . . ."

It is not unlikely that the same situations have taken place in the intervening years since those covered by this recollection. Presidents Truman, Kennedy and Johnson have had their own mixed bag of Democrats to deal with; the Republicans will remember for a long time the acrobatic efforts necessary to hold their own ranks together under the candidacy of Senator Barry Goldwater. Politics is politics.

But whatever local politicos got out of their visits with Roosevelt on his perambulations, the President had his staff see to it that the visits were neither casual nor harmful to the White House; that they must be, in fact, politically profitable. Furthermore, Roosevelt had learned that important stories made public while traveling often had a greater impact than those released routinely in Washington. This manner of releasing stories also gave the

White House at least a few hours of advantage in telling a story in its own way. The items were printed before news bureaus had a chance to do much checking.

This device was used dramatically years later, in 1940, in connection with announcement of the "lending" of a fleet of "overage destroyers" to Britain to aid its fight to keep open life lines on the sea.

There had been a season of disastrous floods in Pennsylvania centering especially on Johnstown. The President took his train on an inspection trip, presumably to dramatize the urgency of flood-control projects in this part of the country by invoking memories of the great disaster that had struck Johnstown half a century earlier. Here was plenty of grist for the news presses, but in an afternoon while reporters were recording these impressions Secretary McIntyre appeared with a sheaf of press releases. The announcement stated that the trade of the destroyers to Britain was being made in exchange for certain rights to defense bases in the western Atlantic. It was the most dramatic news story of that year; it marked a new and very deep commitment in the war then raging in Europe.

Now, it would have been equally easy to release this story in Washington, either through the constantly functioning White House press office, through the State Department, or in a dozen other ways. Yet to release it from the train served two distinct purposes, at least. First, it dramatized and personalized the tag line, "President Roosevelt announced today." Furthermore, no reporter on the spot was equipped with any qualifying background for such an unexpected story, nor could any pick up a telephone to talk with other officials about it.

The stories flashed from the next stop to American newspapers and around the world were precisely the facts announced by the President, in the manner he wished and told in his words. These releases would be printed, and broadcast by radio, immediately upon receipt; if there were critical attacks, qualifications, other detracting statements or changes, they would come later; they could not be published simultaneously. It is a very wise President who mingles his risky foreign policy activities with non-controversial gestures of concern for the people at home.

Roosevelt was a master showman as much as a statesman and all of his successors have used, without finding much room for improvement, techniques that he invented. But he sometimes did get overconfident, and make some laughable if not serious bloopers, by neglecting his research.

On a summer afternoon at Hyde Park, a group of White House staff and reporters were whiling away an afternoon as guests of the President and Mrs. Roosevelt at Val-Kill Cottage, Mrs. Roosevelt's little house. After taking a dip in the small swimming pool, we sat on the lawn waiting for a hot-dog picnic that Mrs. Roosevelt herself was preparing. Whether the subsequent conversation was planned by Roosevelt in advance (as one might think) or was spontaneous, it was one of those no-direct-quotes-but-for-background-only pieces that made up a large part of our dispatches. Covering Roosevelt was somewhat like an assignment to City Hospital; one never knew when something would turn up. We always had to count on the unexpected and prepare for it, even in such an informal atmosphere as an afternoon picnic.

Roosevelt was holding forth, as usual, on the programs and ideals of the New Deal. He talked about the lives of wage-earners, the need for higher standards of minimum wages and better regulation of working conditions in the fringe industries—subjects about which he was surprisingly well informed and with which he had dealt during his tenure as Governor of New York. He said that this was really a lifelong interest, first developed when, "My mother read to me Upton Sinclair's *The Jungle* while I sat at her knees."

From that moment, the reporters present chafed to get to their typewriters. There was very little news during this period, and here was a truly rare story, combining statecraft, human interest and mother lore. I filed a detailed story including even a bit of description of the room at Hyde Park where "Mother" did the reading.

Traveling reporters write the news as they get it and necessarily must carry whatever background they may need in their heads. No reference books are at hand. Consequently I was surprised and embarrassed later in the day, after my office had gotten the story, to receive a telephone call. A copy reader in the office—conscientious, thorough, schooled in the art of research, taking nothing for granted (and possibly a little envious of my glamorous assignment)—greeted me cheerfully, and then asked in bitter-sweet tones: "Just how old was F.D.R. before he stopped sitting at his mother's knees while she read to him?"

Then he explained that *anyone* would know, or could easily verify, that *The Jungle* was published in 1906, at which time Roosevelt was twenty-four years old.

I was not alone. The news agencies have no time to wait for lengthy research on news items. The story was reported all over the country. When queries came in, some explanation was in order. But Roosevelt was no more embarrassed than P. T. Barnum was reported to have been when rain falling on a circus parade washed the white lime off his famous white elephants. The President tilted his cigarette, laughed and commented, "Mother loves to read aloud to all of us."

He knew and we knew that, even allowing for rare lapses of memory or scrambling of facts, much of his charm and political power lay in his skill at improvisation, and that when faced with crises, he was almost "unflappable." He was so confident that we seldom heard him follow line for line the text, distributed in advance, of even major policy speeches. He could interpolate phrases, enlarge upon statements or cut out passages that suddenly seemed dull with such skill that auditors sitting very close to him could not tell by word, pause or gesture that editing was taking place.

Incidentally these talents cost a few papers like *The New York Times* a fortune in telegraph tolls. It is part of the price *The Times* pays for accuracy, and for which it paid highly before radio and television broadcasts lifted sound and visual reporting to their present level.

When Roosevelt was to deliver a prepared speech, *The Times* would always carry—as it does today—the full text. When we had these texts in advance, we handed the complete text to the Western Union operator for transmission to the main office. Then, when the speech was delivered—the lead and news story on it having already been filed—every change had to be wired to the newspaper. Often the changes involved every paragraph, and sometimes this necessitated a rewriting of the news story itself.

Examples of these changes are legion, but the most dramatic one of all—a truly extemporaneous remark— echoed around the world and put into the American language the phrase, "quarantine the aggressors."

Roosevelt had traveled to Chicago to dedicate a bridge, a major showpiece of construction done under the Public Works program started in 1933. He had a fine dedicatory speech prepared in advance in Washington, with all of the proper credits to the PWA and to the Chicago Democratic leaders who might gain some advantage from the occasion. However, the President's mind was much more concerned with mounting clouds on the foreign horizons: Hitler's intransigence, Mussolini's Ethiopian conqu and the civil war raging in Spain. So the President d cided to say a few words, and he did: "quarantine the aggressors."

Within an hour the State Department began to receive inquiries from abroad seeking clarification. In London, newspaper representatives received repeated calls from the foreign office and their British colleagues, asking what this meant. Cabled inquiries to home offices gave no satisfactory answers. And it later developed that Roosevelt probably could not have answered specific questions himself. He just thought it was a good idea—something to throw out for consideration.

But such is the power of a Presidential statement, under certain circumstances and in certain times, that a casual remark can mushroom into world importance.

Anthony Eden, the British Foreign Secretary, issued a call for a Nine-Power Conference at Brussels. Norman Davis was named chairman of the United States Mission. In the end, the Nine-Power Conference became known as the last futile gesture to get the Western powers to show more co-operation for peace-keeping than they had done in the League of Nations.

In 1936, the President gave a superb demonstration not of impetuosity but of self-control under one of the most difficult tests ever caused by his disability.

He had been nominated for re-election by acclamation at the National Democratic Convention in Philadelphia. He traveled to Philadelphia to deliver his acceptance speech in the great stadium there that is best known to the public as the site of the Army-Navy football games. The police estimated that almost eighty thousand persons were waiting to greet him when he arrived.

PART FIVE
Perspective

Perspective

WHEN THE SHOUTING and the voting of 1936 had died away, the New Deal was ended; except for the European dictators, Roosevelt was the most powerful man in the world.

The democratic system of the United States would assert itself later by gradually restricting his peacetime powers, but only in minor matters. Eventually, before 1940, the war in Europe would restore the Presidential power in a pattern the future could not change.

To newspaper reporters—to all observers who were close to the seat of government but not directly involved in it—his power was a phenomenon which occurs only once in many generations. It might have paralleled Abraham Lincoln's and Woodrow Wilson's power had they survived their moments of victory, but they did not. Roosevelt did survive his New Deal, and he led the country through the war years long enough to leave that accretion of power as a heritage to his successors.

Had the United States experienced reasonable economic recovery up to 1940, without the intervention of war, Roosevelt might never have been chosen for a third term. But in 1937 he stood at the pinnacle of both power and popularity, yet on a slippery platform being greased by the small but determined group of national leaders who already thought he had gone too far.

Jim Farley made his precise guess as to the extent of Roosevelt's second-term victory because—whether he or another said it first—in 1936 "everybody was against Roosevelt except the people."

This was more than a prescient wisecrack. Almost every segment of industry and business—the leaders of which had backed Roosevelt so enthusiastically in 1932—was disenchanted.

The New Deal taxes and deficits seemed to these thoughtful men to be threatening the economy with inflation, if not collapse. They found themselves not only taxed and taxed, but submerged in paper work, reports and regulations often compared with the *dicta* laid down by the German and Italian dictatorships. What had been confidential business records for generations became the subject of intense scrutiny by regulating officials. Individual proprietors and family business owners complained that they worked all week and spent the week ends making out records and reports.

The financial community was distressed and sometimes panicked. Government control over currency and debts and regulation of the securities and commodity exchanges had taken almost all initiative and responsibility from the financial centers and had vested it in Washington.

Earlier New Deal stalwarts in the Senate, including Glass and Byrd, had become critics of Roosevelt's financial and budget policies—particularly his espousal of "foreign theories." He was accused of being hoodwinked by the theories of the British economist Maynard Keynes, who held that inflation and government debt can, under some circumstances, help the national economy; not ruin it.

Bankers who had welcomed a limited guarantee of deposits by the government, to reassure their depositors, now began to chafe at the additional regulations and examinations imposed upon them. Communities that fought for their share of public works saw the organization of groups that deplored this expenditure of federal funds. The same organizations often took stands in one instance in favor of enlarged Federal aid to their own communities but opposed to the measures used to finance these projects.

It was estimated that, on the basis of public opinion polls, newspapers holding approximately ninety per cent of all circulation were opposed editorially to Roosevelt's major policies.

But the *people* were for him. Who were the people?

Some few supporters may have been recipients of direct relief payments, but not many of them were in the same area long enough to vote under residential qualifications. By and large, the mass of New Deal support did come from solid citizens, although not from the community "leaders." They were the home owners with mortgages guaranteed against foreclosure; wage-earners enjoying a minimum wage that would seem absurdly low a few years later but in 1936 represented security; small independent merchants whose weekly fortunes fluctuated with the buying power of these individuals; and the smaller farmers whose incomes were increased by agricultural programs as opposed to the larger land owners whose taxes offset their "benefits."

Moreover, millions of urban and rural dwellers, who were not directly affected monetarily by these programs, watched gladly while their savings and the economic surroundings reflected general improvement. They approved of the programs for land reclamation, public power projects, flood control and the massive programs developing everything from warships to bridges and highways.

In other words, the New Deal received its second victory at the hands of the voiceless ones, the unorganized millions who had no business organizations or labor unions to speak for them in the Washington lobbies, but who could vote. Few of these read or debated the reports in the financial pages or the editorial columns of the metropolitan newspapers, which often insisted that "recovery" had come about through the play of "natural forces."

They did not care for such arguments, if they even could understand them. Neither were they concerned with the petulant statements by New Deal spokesmen that older and conservative institutions—notably the Supreme Court —were still a drag on the plans for progress. They judged their benefits more by instinct, and continued to tune their radios faithfully to Roosevelt's "fireside chats."

Thus this President got his second mandate and plunged ahead, although there was ever-increasing high-level opposition, even from many in his own party. There came, too, at this time, a notable change in attitudes toward him by many former followers. Perhaps this disenchantment was the normal reaction to overadulation, or it was resentment from those who felt the Administration owed them something. It was equally true that many early antagonists of the New Deal had come to the conclusion that Roosevelt had made a real contribution to America. Not all thoughtful people were opposed to him; neither did he hold the unquestioning loyalty of all those groups his program had helped the most.

His overwhelming victory over Alf M. Landon may have fooled even him at the time. It seems inevitable that he would have won against any opponent, but the Republican nomination of Landon—honest, sincere, dull, unimaginative and not even able to hold an audience with a speech—made the Roosevelt technique twice as effective as it would have been otherwise. Strangely enough, the anti-Roosevelt groups realized this immediately after the election in 1936. Some of them seemed to understand that, although they accused Roosevelt of pursuing the course of "dictatorship," they themselves had contributed as much as his supporters to the enhancement of his power.

The President felt this opposition, but his reaction was to make a fight of it, rather than compromise; and the American public saw a new and more forceful President than the great unifier of his first Administration.

The former sympathetic figure, the crippled crusader determined to serve his country despite his handicaps, now was a battling politician seemingly standing on his own two feet. When the public saw him in newsreels, they saw a vigorous man, with powerful shoulders and jutting jaw, seated behind a desk. In public appearances, he stood erect on braced legs that minimized any suggestion of physical infirmity. No one any longer thought that critics of the President were taking unfair pot shots at a cripple, and he more than anyone else contributed to that feeling.

Then, there came the questions—sometimes asked with intended malice and other times with honest confusion—about the President's mental stability. Had his physical affliction affected his mind?

All of these questions created many bitter debates prior to the reunification of the country behind Roosevelt after Pearl Harbor. Underlying these conflicting feelings, in 1936, was the attitude that the Depression really was a thing of the past—that the country would settle down eventually to some form of normalcy without new controls. This speculation skirted several basic questions concerning the change. For one thing, many of the New

Deal programs, from Social Security to agricultural relief, had been accepted. More arguments still prevailed
in the field of public power development. The extent of
continued business and finance regulation was also a
matter of controversy, as was industry-labor bargaining.
In the ranks of labor itself, John L. Lewis was flaying
with all his eloquence the "broken promises" of the
Roosevelt Administration.

There was argument, it seemed, over the New Deal in
every quarter. This kept Roosevelt on the political defen-
sive but—and this is an important *but*—his critics were so
various that they could not unify against him.

Southern statesmen fulminated against the accretion of
power in Washington and the intrusion by northern political leaders on their States rights, but none bolted to the
Republican Party. John L. Lewis led the critical labor
wing, but the friendlier attitude of William L. Green
nullified his effectiveness; and neither labor wing joined
forces with, for instance, the United States Chamber of
Commerce. Western farm leaders criticized the agricultural programs for their alleged inadequacy but none
joined the city "bosses" in common cause for universally
greater benefits for the poor.

Most ironic of all the phases of the domestic hodge-
podge were the self-virtuous denunciations by State and
regional groups of the Federal spending programs in an
era that saw the first development of organized offices and
pressure groups in Washington to obtain ever greater
shares of the handouts.

In the center of this maelstrom, apparently growing
calmer and more toughened to criticism, sat Roosevelt.
His criticisms of his own detractors diminished, and less
time was spent on answering them. After 1936 and his
whirlwind series of "inspection tours," he traveled less
frequently. His staff set up higher barriers to fend off

importunate callers. After the 1937 Inaugural, Roosevelt seemed to turn inward, and to feel that he need spend less time in open political combat.

Within two years the preoccupation of European war and America's subsequent involvements entirely changed the picture. The issues became international, and not contentions over the New Deal. Then, Roosevelt's strongest opponents arose in the ranks of the isolationists, but these people never unified. His Presidential Republican opponent in 1940 was Wendell L. Willkie, who seemed to vie with Roosevelt for the very causes for which Roosevelt stood.

Thus the New Deal merged into the American tradition, almost by default; no longer a gay adventure or even a lingering matter of debate.

Erected on a new social and economic basis in Roosevelt's first term, it weathered most shocks in the second. In the third, it was all but forgotten in the massive effort of the war. After peace, it was the relatively old and respected foundation for the modern American way of life.

There probably would come, at some time, another crusade and another leader chosen by the voters to work out comparable radical changes in government.

But from that recent and yet almost historic past of 1932 to 1936 there came again the lesson the United States has so often reviewed, and as often forgotten. Changes are part of the rule in development of our own unique form of government, but when changes do occur they spring from new ideas. None has yet succeeded in turning back the clock.

Index

Index prepared by Lyn Hayes.

A HAWTHORN BOOK